THE POWER OF US:

The Art and Science of
Enlightened Citizen Engagement
and Collective Action

---

*How the US Government "Really" Works and
How to Get It to Work for You*

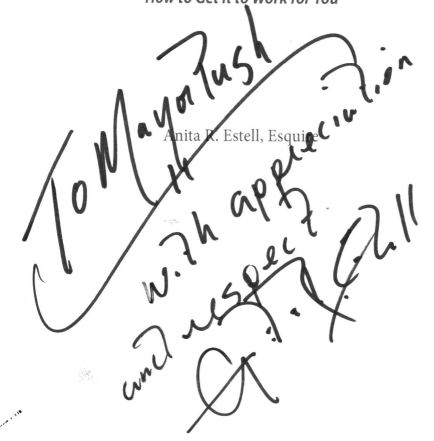

Anita R. Estell, Esquire

AuthorHouse™ LLC
1663 Liberty Drive
Bloomington, IN 47403
www.authorhouse.com
Phone: 1-800-839-8640

Published by AuthorHouse   09/23/2014

ISBN: 978-1-4817-1556-0 (sc)
ISBN: 978-1-4817-1555-3 (hc)
ISBN: 978-1-4817-1554-6 (e)

Library of Congress Control Number: 2013903433

For my mother, Flora Estell, and Aunt Avery Orr
and those members of your family and mine who
sacrificed blood, sweat, and tears for freedom,
expanded opportunities, and the pursuit of excellence.

CONTENTS

Section One: Thoughts, Words, Deeds, and Enlightened Citizen Engagement

Section Two: Information and Resources for
Persons of Passion and Vision

Section Three: Appendices

Appendix I: Other Key Internet Resources 106

    Budget and Appropriations 106

    Lobbyist Information 107

More

FOREWORD

For some, *The Power of Us* provides a new perspective; for others, it provides a reminder of basic themes unique to America and our way of living; for still others, it serves as a marker for a new beginning. Whatever the case, it is a must-read for those who want to know more about how the federal government works. For those who understand the relevance of living now and the need for expanded engagement at the national level, look no further. At its core, *The Power of Us* reflects Estell's understanding that ultimately, the power is with the people.

Americans live in an incredibly diverse nation and are a part of an even more diverse global community. As members, we have a right not only to make a living but also to live a good life, at peace with neighbors across the street and across the ocean. Decisions made and not made in Washington, DC have profound implications for us all.

Where Are We and Where Are We Going?

The American form of government has proven itself to be a masterful piece of machinery pressing toward freedom's peaks and sidestepping or overcoming any valleys that would derail freedom's promise. Today, we find ourselves living in extraordinary times accompanied by infinite opportunities. New developments and inventions rivet our imagination and increase our access to information almost daily. Global trends, new industries and applications, and shifting demographics require adaptation and forward thinking. They also require us to refocus our attention on how we engage with Washington and the federal process. There is much truth in the expression "We came here on different ships, but we are all in the same boat now." Far more than in the past, many people are reaching beyond communities that look like them, and a keen sense of curiosity has sprung up regarding the workings of government and how any one of us can become involved. It has been affirmed that we, the people, matter. We can make a difference. We can fuel change. Now what?

The challenges our communities face require nothing short of the expanded engagement of a diverse group of citizens, including both those familiar with government and those who have never taken their efforts to or beyond the voting booth. Moving forward boldly is the only reasonable option. The luxury of time has escaped us, and as the old folks would say in the community where I grew up, "We have a hard row to hoe, but we've got to hoe it."

This book is relevant and timely. During no other time in our history have so many folks, on such a large scale, recognized the need to engage and connect in the interest of a common good. We are, as the Rev. Martin Luther King Jr. once said, "caught in an inescapable network of mutuality, tied in a single garment of destiny." *The Power of Us* provides the information required to respond to a fundamental question about who must be engaged in bringing about the change we need and deserve in our nation: If not us, then who?

Johnnetta Betsch Cole
*President Emerita, Spelman College
and Bennett College for Women*

ABOUT THIS HANDBOOK

What happens in Washington, DC, affects every aspect of American life, including the quality of the air we breathe, the water we drink, the food we eat, and so much more. This book recognizes established principles that affirm all people are of equal value and have a right to be represented and to engage in the American process of government. The essence of its core proposition is that we—the people—really matter and ultimately rule. There is no USA without "us."

Stories of real people who successfully engaged at the national level appear in these pages. The point to take away is that the most successful efforts are not government-run programs but those that engage communities and individuals as champions, business and civic leaders, philanthropists, supporters, and volunteers holding the government accountable along the way. More important, it is one thing to participate, petition, and protest at the national level but quite another to be effective at the national level.

The Power of Us provides practical instruction on how to tap into this power and use it as leverage. Essentially a two-step process, it's as much about who we are at the core of our essence, our "human being-ness," as it is about what we do. Much of the secret lies in the first step: believing that we have the power, owning that power as ours to have, and using it in a way that is compassionate and respectful of the value of human life. And then, for the second step, we must become familiar with the basics: how the federal government is organized, how to become more effectively engaged at the local and national levels, and what to do and where to go to connect more effectively with and to influence Congress, the White House, and federal agencies.

This handbook is divided into three main sections: Section One: Thoughts, Words, Deeds, and Enlightened Engagement; Section Two: Information and Resources for Persons of Passion and Vision; and Section Three: Appendices.

Section One contains six chapters and addresses how to put ideas into action as a matter of law, how the seeds of change are within each of us, and how the fruits of democracy, be they bitter or sweet, are a manifestation of who we are as individuals and communities of interests. Questions you will be able to answer include:

Can my idea really become law?

What does it take to get noticed in Washington?

Is it just me, or has politics taken a turn for the worse?

The political climate is so toxic; can I really make a difference? How do I get started?

Section Two contains four chapters, and questions answered include:

How can I get a meeting with my senator or representative? What do I need to know to make a trip to Washington?

How do I plan for a trip, and who should go with me?

What should I say when I meet, speak to, or write my representative or senator?

Where can I go to learn about a particular agency program? How can I contact the president, first lady, White House, or a particular agency?

Section Three provides a compilation of essays that provide supplementary guidance. Some of the questions this section answers are:

Where can I learn about the federal budget process?

Where can I look up a federal law or legislation?

As contestants on national music competition shows are encouraged to "make a song their own," I have done my best to present a perspective and understanding of the role of a citizen that stands out as "my own" but which honors those who have shared vital philosophies, writings, policies, and teachings as well as those who love, listen, and move to freedom's rhythm and flow.

PREFACE

A New Day

I was born in 1959, and grew up during the early days of the civil rights movement, one of the most tumultuous and transformational eras in US history. I was articulate and communicative from a young age, reciting my first memorized poem, "Jesus Wept," in church at age four. At the risk of sounding boastful, I can say that by second grade, my leadership, writing and speaking skills had been noticed by adults and students. In junior high, I won a seat on the student council, and co-founded an underground newspaper. By high school, I fully blossomed into your basic Type A overachiever whose evolving activism was stoked by Mahatma Gandhi, Henry David Thoreau, and Dr. Martin Luther King Jr. Apartheid in South Africa opened my eyes to global racism. Thoreau's *Civil Disobedience* revealed the import of casting "your whole vote, not a strip of paper merely, but your whole influence," and *Walden* drove home the truth, "What lies behind us and what lies ahead of us are tiny matters compared to what lives within us."

In some ways, King, Gandhi and Thoreau were my high school guidance counselors. Ignoring conventional divides between rich and poor, black and white, urban and rural, Christian and non-Christian, I became a bridge builder and student leader bent on dismantling existing walls and striding through previously closed doors of opportunity. Debate teams, beauty pageants, oration contests, all were major events, and by winning many of them, I earned many "firsts" for my family and community.

Arriving at the University of Missouri-Columbia in 1977, I ignited a firestorm by rushing the all-white sororities and challenging taboo campus racial issues that had festered for decades. I became a "go-to" student voice, joined the student anti-apartheid movement, pressing for US disinvestment in South Africa, and feminist efforts, demanding rights for women around the globe. If that weren't enough, I worked part-time, consistently made the dean's list, qualified for the honors college, earned a bachelor's in journalism and a juris doctor, and passed the state bar on the first try. At 27, I was a licensed attorney.

Trailblazing and bridge building are part of my DNA. I had my first passionate date with destiny when I discovered that in Washington, DC, I actually could make a living shaping laws and policies to help the folks I cared about. Working for the US House of Representatives' Committee on Appropriations for Congressman Louis Stokes provided valuable insights into the federal budget, particularly programs for community development, consumer product safety, education, environment, health, human services, housing, labor, science, and veterans affairs. Capitol Hill is the world's best classroom for learning how government works, or doesn't, and how communities can connect to the process and to each other. The greatness of a democracy is measured by the level of constructive engagement of its people in working together for their mutual benefit.

Bold Endeavors

When I left the Hill, colleagues urged me to "do something different as a lobbyist," to bring a new face and philosophy to the national scene. After a brief stint in the Clinton administration as a senior advisor to the secretary of education, Richard Riley, I got serious about "cause advocacy," lobbying, and promoting social issues, diverse stakeholder groups and underserved communities. My success rate rivaled that of more heavily financed special interests. Over two decades, I have helped nonprofit and public sector clients craft federal policies that have benefited millions of people, and yielded billions of dollars in programs nationwide.

The relevance and role of the private sector in driving innovation, job creation and community revitalization, took on new meaning as I successfully worked with corporate clients to underwrite the development and distribution of HIV/AIDS drugs; worked with private equity firms to expand opportunities in emerging domestic markets; and helped broker a $21.6 billion multinational merger-and-acquisition deal.

A casual observer might assume I have "made it," with a resume that includes a congressional committee appointment, a presidential appointment, pioneering lobbying work, and equity ownership of a national law firm. I have worked successfully with White House teams, cabinet secretaries, governors, mayors, celebrities, corporate and nonprofit CEOs and top philanthropists. I have reveled in the unparalleled achievements of movements and groups working for the greater good, and was honored to advocate for civil rights icon Rosa Parks at the national level for her cherished nonprofit bearing her name and in support of the many honors she received following her death.

The journey has been grand, but much work remains until all the world's citizens have the opportunity to do better and be better. Throughout my life, my eyes have seen the stories of the unwanted, neglected, abandoned and abused, as well as the achievements of the informed, enlightened and empowered. I have seen the sweet successes associated with people working for the greater good. The best part of the American story is the resiliency of its people. These are the folks who dare to reach and climb in the face of burdens, baggage, and calamities. Resiliency, action and resolve have worked for countless millions from across the generations.

No day is promised, but each day we fail to address relevant issues at the local and national level, real people with real needs suffer. Much of the work to ease their burdens falls to federal policymakers, and to each of us as citizens.

The philosophies and observations I share in this book meld lessons in professional best practices, case studies and techniques acquired over a lifetime, including 27 years in Washington, DC. Having worked with national and grassroots activists, private citizens and corporate interests of every political stripe—conservatives, moderates and progressives—this book embraces diverse viewpoints. As an attorney and journalist, I have scrupulously tried to attribute and credit the statements and research of others, but when I speak in the first person, I am sharing personal stories and experiences.

My Truth

It is my hope that this work informs, inspires and calls you to action to engage powerfully and collectively with others. We can overcome daunting odds when we work together. Through love, faith, and thoughtful plans for constructive action, good works and endurance, we can dissolve the barriers that promote suffering and realize our true human and civic potential. This, friends, is my truth. I pray that what I share here brings you closer to discovering and realizing yours. If I may assist in your journey, please reach out to me at www.anitaestell.com.

SECTION ONE

Thoughts, Words, Deeds, and Enlightened Citizen Engagement

CHAPTER 1
Putting Ideas into Action
Nothing happens until something moves. — Albert Einstein

E = MC² . . . in politics, too

Albert Einstein tops the list of modern revolutionaries; the man and his ideas were a game changer. Today, we classify him as a genius, which is even more fascinating when you consider he started his career as a locksmith and, as a child, was called the "dopey one" because he was a slow learner. Einstein considered impudence a virtue and has been described as a reverential revolutionary. According to Walter Isaacson in *Einstein: His Life and Universe*:

> His success came from questioning conventional wisdom, challenging authority and marveling at mysteries that struck others as mundane. This led him to embrace a morality and politics based on respect for free minds, free spirits and free individuals. Tyranny repulsed him, and he saw tolerance not simply as a sweet virtue but as a necessary condition for a creative society.

One of Einstein's more popular equations is relevant to our advocacy discussion: $E = MC^2$, or energy equals mass times the square of the speed of light. The speed of light's ascribed value is exactly 299,792,458 meters per second, or approximately 300,000 kilometers per second, which is about 186,000 miles per second. That's pretty darn fast. In fact, it would take about 70 coast-to-coast trips from Washington, DC to Los Angeles to cover 186,000 miles. Taking this number to the second power is even more fascinating. Consequently, according to Einstein, a tiny amount of matter has an extraordinary impact when converted completely into energy. Clarifying the complexities of Einstein's equation related to speed and mass, Isaacson notes in his book on Einstein the energy in the mass of one raisin could supply most of New York City's energy requirements for one day. Imagine that!

Drop, Ripple, and Tide

Turning to people, there have been numerous instances in our history when we have come together and unleashed our energies as individuals, communities, and nations. I refer to these scenarios as "drop, ripple, and tide." Consider, for example, that in its liquid state, water is a powerful force. It is most powerful when in motion. Individual action can be compared to a drop of water, which can create a ripple, and a ripple a tide. Likewise, in politics, nothing happens until something moves. The larger the mass, the more impact a movement has when energized and unleashed. Within the American context, the mass is the people, as in "the masses." The American political, social, and economic landscapes often have been influenced by a multiplicity of individual and collective voices that have, on one hand, reflected the ingenuity and life-affirming mind-set required to accomplish the most extraordinary innovations and achievements. On the other hand, massed voices sometimes have discordant tones, defiant and intolerant of opposing views. Real progress is achieved when the collective energy of like-minded people is carefully synchronized and constructively engaged.

In *The Biology of Belief: Unleashing the Power of Consciousness, Matter, and Miracles,* author Bruce L. Lipton, PhD, presents two scenarios of what happens when a pebble is dropped into a pond. First, the falling pebble has energy because of the force of gravity pulling on its mass. Once the pebble hits the water, the energy of the pebble in motion is transmitted to the water, and the ripples generated by the pebble are actually energy waves passing through the water. When more than one pebble is tossed into the water at the same time, Lipton writes, the spreading ripples (energy waves) from each stone can interfere with one another, creating composite waves when two or more ripples converge. This type of interference is either constructive (energy amplifying) or destructive (energy deflating). As a cell biologist, Lipton explains this phenomenon in this way:

> Dropping two pebbles of the same size, from the same height and at exactly the same time, coordinates the wave action of their ripples. The ripples from each pebble converge on each other. Where the ripples overlap, the combined power of the interacting waves is doubled—a phenomenon referred to as constructive interference, or harmonic resonance. When the dropping of the pebbles is not coordinated, their energy waves are out of sync. As one wave is going up, the other is going down. At the point of convergence these out of sync energy waves cancel each other . . . the water is calm . . . there is no energy wave. This phenomenon of canceling energy waves is called destructive interference.

Political movements resemble pebbles landing in a pond. There have been times when people from different walks of life with similar mind-sets have come together at the same place and at the same time, like ripples in freedom's waters, to generate great waves of opportunity and achievement. Recall the Rev. Dr. Martin Luther King's "I Have a Dream" speech, in which he proclaimed that those involved with the march toward freedom would not be satisfied until justice rolled down like water and righteousness like a mighty stream. Clearly, we are not pebbles, yet we know from science, philosophy, and religion that the energy associated with our beliefs, thoughts, words, and deeds defines the magnificence (or lack thereof) of any movement. We have the ability to make waves.

I appreciate also the observations of Malcolm Gladwell, author of *The Tipping Point: How Little Things Can Make a Big Difference.* Gladwell notes the relevance of "believing change is possible" and "the right kind of impetus." He concludes that the bedrock force that underlies successful social epidemics is a belief that change is possible. This belief must be embraced by individuals who, in the face of the right kind of impetus, choose to transform their behavior or beliefs. He notes the following:

> Merely by manipulating the size of a group, we can dramatically improve its receptivity to new ideas. By tinkering with the presentation of information, we can significantly improve its stickiness. Simply by finding and reaching those few special people who hold so much social power, we can shape the course of social epidemics. In the end, tipping points are a reaffirmation of the potential for change and the power of intelligent action. Look at the world around you. It may seem like an immovable, implacable place. It is not. With the slightest push—in just the right place—it can be tipped.

CHAPTER 2

The Power Within

Be the change that you want to see in the world. —Mahatma Gandhi

In delivering the invocation for the second inauguration of Barack Obama, the 44th president of the United States, Myrlie Evers-Williams, the widow of the late civil rights leader Medgar Evers, invoked the collective wisdom of our grandmothers and eloquently articulated the relevance of the power within. In referring to those wise women who came before us, she said:

> 'God make me a blessing.' Let their spirit guide us as we claim the spirit of old. There's something within me that holds the reins. There's something within me that banishes pain. There's something within me I cannot explain. But all I know America, there is something within. There is something within.

There is a power within each of us to effect change and to promote freedom and justice. People make laws. Laws do not make people. Even you can make a law. In a compilation of writings selected and published by the late Coretta Scott King (a contemporary of Evers-Williams), the words of Rev. Dr. Martin Luther King Jr. also remind us:

> Everybody can be great because anybody can serve. You don't have to have a college degree to serve. You don't have to make your subject and your verb agree to serve. You don't have to know about Plato and Aristotle to serve. You don't have to know Einstein's theory of relativity to serve. You don't have to know the second theory of thermodynamics in physics to serve. You only need a heart full of grace. A soul generated by love.

While there are many definitions of power, it is essentially the energy that enables us to help ourselves and others and to influence the world around us. Real power, as Dr. King suggests, is associated with helping others and, as Evers-Williams observed, comes from within.

For the purposes of this discussion, there are two types of power. The first and most sustainable is in the alignment and fusion of FLOW, which stands for faith, love, opportunity, and will.[1]

---

[1] The term *will* as used here refers to purposeful, personal passion and assuredness. It is that inner force produced by the collision of intentionality, courage, and endurance (ICE); it both anchors and unleashes our essence, bringing into formation the substance of our dreams. All elements of ICE are important, but the importance of endurance when working at the national level cannot be overestimated. Remember, the race is not won by the strong or the swift but by the one who endures to the end.

Power Point ⇨ Another Take on the Power of FLOW

The power of FLOW is the same thing that author Gary Zukav calls "authentic power" in his book *The Seat of the Soul*. Authentic power, he observes, occurs "when we align our thoughts, emotions, and actions with the highest part of ourselves." In those instances, "we are filled with enthusiasm, purpose, and meaning. . . . We have no thoughts of bitterness." According to Zukav, "Authentic power has its roots in the deepest source of our being. [It] cannot be bought, inherited or hoarded."

Another type of power, a more destructive type, is the power of FLOP, which stands for fear, loathing, obstructionism, and pessimism. FLOW and FLOP essentially are two sides of the same coin. The nature of how we engage as citizens and leaders, the type of thinking and energy we bring, determines the outcome of the coin toss. Insertion of FLOW or FLOP into the power equation (discussed next) totally changes the impact an advocacy or public policy effort will have on communities.

The power equation represents key elements of an advocacy plan, and is articulated as follows: Vision × Knowledge × Power × n(PEACE) = Change. In this equation, n(PEACE) stands for — the number of persons engaged and affected changes everything.[2] The clearer the vision and the greater the knowledge, power, and number of people engaged and affected, the greater and more impactful the success. See the power equation visual below.

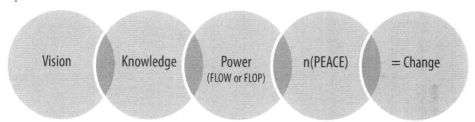

Vision   Knowledge   Power (FLOW or FLOP)   n(PEACE)   = Change

Every industry and sector can point to persons who have made lasting and powerful contributions. Like the many classifications of power, civic engagement also comes in several forms. I call them *law abiding, advocate,* and *revolutionary*. As you read the following descriptions, ask yourself which best describes you.

Law-abiding citizens possess elected power. Persons in this category are trying to make it on their own, and they live from day to day and often from paycheck to paycheck. Law-abiding citizens are people who obey the law and may be willing to take a case to court to resolve disputes if they have the energy, time, and resources necessary to do so. They may or may not vote regularly, and they have never contacted an elected

---

[2] David R. Hawkins, MD, PhD, *Power vs. Force: The Hidden Determinants of Human Behavior* (Carlsbad, CA: Hay House, 2002), 102. This power equation represents a logarithmic (and not an arithmetic) progression of calibrated power levels, whereby individual choice plays a key role and human action motivated by compassion, kindness, and charity ranks high on the energy scale.

official. They work from a power source defined by acceptance, which is the same as acquiescence.

Advocates possess connected power. These are people who leverage their knowledge and relationships by joining movements or otherwise mobilize as individuals and communities in support of (or in opposition to) a particular issue. As Roger Hamilton notes, "Once we begin to share our power with others, we begin to shift to connected power." Activities may connect through family, work, synagogue, mosque, church, or charity, and their activities may include building coalitions, and organizing boycotts, petitions, or voter registration drives. Persons falling into this group move with an energy marked by enjoyment.

A **revolutionary** exhibits a reverence for life and has reflected power that has the strongest impact and achieves results that are indelible and sustainable. These persons align and leverage character and purpose and engage in a way that influences, defines, and drives the establishment of law and policy that transforms communities and nations, even after they have died. These people are thinkers, innovators, and doers whose power is marked by zeal, a profound understanding of the forces that connect us all, and the ability through their efforts to improve the quality of life for masses of folks. This power, by definition, is derived from a higher source. Those falling into this group have tenacity and unwavering enthusiasm and passion for their cause.

SPECIFIC EXAMPLES:

Law Abiding

My mother was big on being law abiding. As a divorced mom of seven, she was obsessed with making sure we stayed out of trouble. We knew to avoid hitting people,

VISION x	KNOWLEDGE x	POWER x (FLOW or FLOP)	n (PEACE)	= Change
Different Types of Citizenship	Law abiding (Basic Compliance)	Elected: Accept	1	Comply with the status quo and whatever the government requires. Limited reach and impact.
	Advocate (Explore & Expand)	Connected: Enjoy	2 or more	Connect with others to effect change at the family, work, grassroots, & national levels. Power ceases upon disconnection or death.
	Revolutionary (Innovate & Create)	Reflected: Enthused	Hundreds to millions	Create opportunities for large numbers of people, even after death.

to pay for items before leaving the store, and to never put anything in our pockets or otherwise conceal anything that didn't belong to us. As we started driving, her warnings extended to obeying traffic laws, coming home on time, choosing the right friends, and staying away from drugs and people who used them. As a law-abiding citizen, my mother always filed her taxes on time, and we looked forward to getting a refund. When the restaurant where she worked burned, we learned about unemployment benefits, food stamps, free lunch cards, and "government cheese." Though we didn't have much, we always shared; we knew many families who had less than we did.

Advocates

My political interest started in the '60s and '70s when I watched my mother blaze a trail in her leaky, creaky, smoke-spewing '57 Chevy. It was all about GOTV, get out the vote. Period. My mother and community embraced GOTV with a zealousness that seemed as sacred as life itself. I rode shotgun, helping seniors translate their hope and faith into a tangible vote at the polls. For many back then and now, voting was and is perceived as the end all and be all. Elected officials can always be voted out of office if they fail to address our concerns. However, throwing the bums out is an exhausting, chaotic, and costly process. Voters must realize that electing someone is just a first step. Another real opportunity for influence comes after the polls close. Experienced advocates recognize the relevance of taking advantage of existing laws, influencing decisions in making laws, and spending taxpayer money after those elected take office. They understand the need and embrace the opportunity to strategically check in with elected officials to remind them of priorities and to hold them accountable. Advocates know that whatever policymakers are working on should be what they were elected to do.

True Story: Connect. Leverage. Build. During a prolonged season of historically high unemployment levels, congressional gridlock, and a stalled presidential jobs package in the fall of 2011, Starbucks announced the launch of a jobs-creation initiative that exploited laws already on the books and a program that had been in place at the Department of Treasury for many years. The company (providing $5 million in seed capital) partnered with the Opportunity Finance Network (OFN), which is the national network of Community Development Financial Institutions (CDFI). Using donations and public and private resources, the network is responsible for making more than $23 billion in loans to businesses located in low-income and low-wealth communities. Announced on October 3, 2011, Create Jobs for USA places donations from Starbucks customers, partners (employees), and concerned citizens into a nationwide fund, managed by OFN, for community business lending.

Outcome: This venture leverages public and private resources to extend their reach and impact to promote job creation in the United States. It leverages the strengths of the CDFI program, the experience of OFN, and the goodwill and power of Starbucks and a relevant base, the people (customers and employees). As of October 2012, the Create Jobs for USA website reported an expected 5,000 jobs were created or retained as a result of this initiative.

Revolutionary

New media make keeping track of politics much easier. But knowing and doing are different things. You see, the process of drafting and adopting federal laws and policies is simply a manifestation of what we believe and intend to do as individuals within a nation. Through individual and collective engagement, elected officials are held accountable and programs consistent with the will of those who engage are implemented. Now, take a moment to acknowledge that your opinions matter. You can make a difference. Many popular laws originate from the ideas and work of people who have never been involved with the government, but they have recognized a need and have taken steps to address it. You say, "Uh-uh." I say, "Really."

True story: Lilly Ledbetter worked for a Gadsden, Alabama, tire and rubber manufacturer for almost twenty years. By 1997, at nearly the age of sixty, she was an area manager, the only woman to hold that position. Fifteen male peers made more money than she did, and the gap was huge: Ledbetter earned $3,727 a month; the lowest-paid man got $4,286, and the highest-paid man got $5,236 a month. Ledbetter sued, and her case ultimately reached the US Supreme Court. In *Ledbetter vs. Goodyear Tire & Rubber Co.*, decided May 2007, the court ruled she had waited too long, well beyond the 180-day statute of limitations, finding "she could have and should have sued." Since this was the Supreme Court, you might think that was that. But it wasn't. In our checks-and-balances system, Congress came through and passed a law effectively reversing the court's decision.

Outcome: The Lilly Ledbetter Fair Pay Act was signed into law on January 29, 2009. The bill amends the Civil Rights Act of 1964 and requires the 180-day statute of limitations to reset with each new discriminating paycheck.

True story: On January 13, 1996, nine-year-old Amber Hagerman rode her bike in an abandoned parking lot near her grandparents' home in Arlington, Texas. A man in a black pickup truck pulled up and grabbed her. Four days later, Amber's body was found near a creek bed. She had been molested and her throat was cut.

Outcome: The law and alert system we know as Amber Alert came out of this tragedy. Amber's family and neighbors engaged the media, eventually asking their congressman to introduce legislation to strengthen federal penalties for anyone convicted of molesting a child. Amber's family wanted to "make sure this doesn't happen to anyone else's little girl," according to former US Representative Martin Frost, who introduced the Amber Hagerman Child Protection Act. Frost then worked with law enforcement officials in the Dallas-Fort Worth area to establish the Amber Alert, later taken nationwide in legislation he successfully sponsored because he listened to voters. In a note shared by Frost with me, he said,

> All this happened as a direct result of a group of citizens in my district who were upset by the crime that was committed and who then asked their con-

gressman to get laws passed in Washington to prevent similar things from happening to other children. Citizens talking to their congressman about a particular problem that they think needs to be remedied can make a big difference. Members of Congress respond to voters in the district, particularly about issues that involve families and public safety.

CHAPTER 3
Believe

E ducating and familiarizing yourself with Washington and the federal process is not as hard as it might seem. The first time around, understanding what to do and where to go can be confusing and intimidating. But, almost anyone can be effective after studying the issue, outlining a plan, and enlisting help from supporters and champions. Never be afraid to admit what you don't know, and ask for advice. That's what we pay those who are elected to do—help.

Power Line: Transforming Ideas into Policy

Good ideas don't get a welcoming party in Washington, and great ideas often are buried alive. Even so, don't be discouraged. There are many who have made a mark. Those who make an impression, and eventually an impact, have some common characteristics, and they successfully connect the five steps that comprise the power line. It is through the use of the power line that ideas are transformed into federal policies that actually touch the lives of real people. Basically, the five steps (from idea to policy) are the following:

Discover: Generate, imagine, and unveil ideas that address the needs of individuals and communities.

Develop: Take steps to bring an idea from latency to fulfillment or implementation.

Innovate: Pursue a new approach (or an old approach with a new twist) to support the idea's implementation.

Aggregate: Bring multiple players of like minds together around a common cause.

Sustain and Scale: Maintain a viable presence and the ability to produce a desired effect for many people for many years.

Discover ■ Develop ■ Innovate ■ Aggregate ■ Sustain and Scale

It is relevant to note that the five steps associated with the power line align with the five factors that comprise the power equation.

VISION x	KNOWLEDGE x	POWER x (FLOW or FLOP)	n (PEACE)	= Change
Discover ➡	Develop ➡	Innovate ➡	Aggregate ➡	Sustain & Scale

Power Characteristics

People who are successful at the federal level also share some common characteristics that correlate to the elements of the power line and power equation. The most successful persons are able to visualize and commit; know the issue; have faith in or sense of connection to a power bigger than them; coalesce and engage; and persevere and lay a foundation.

IMAGINE, VISUALIZE & COMMIT	Using your mind's eye, find your north star; see what you want to achieve, and commit yourself to obtaining it.
KNOW THE ISSUE & PLAN	Research the issue and steps needed to reach your goal. Develop a plan.
PLUG INTO THE SOURCE AND FLOW	Recognize that there is a power that is bigger than all of us but available to any of us. Plug into the Source, using the principles of FLOW.
COALESCE, COMMUNICATE & ENGAGE	Enlist other stakeholders and elected leaders and take definitive action. Identify any opposition.
PERSEVERE & LAY A FOUNDATION	Make sure your efforts benefit future generations and can be sustained over time, if appropriate.

Ask yourself what you have a burning desire to do, fix, or influence. You can dream big or try to tackle something that affects you or your community personally, like the family that made the Amber Alert possible or like Lilly Ledbetter. Are there some homeless, elderly, sick, or disabled folks you want to help? Do you want college to be more affordable or to see banking reforms? Would you like incentives for small business, or do you see an environmental concern screaming for a remedy? Check your gut. True north is always the issue that moves you most deeply and represents a breath of creation—hope. Be prepared to commit the time, energy, and resources to achieve your goal. Take a position, and then stay focused. While every American can tap into these strengths, some individuals and efforts I have encountered broaden the definition of extraordinary. Think Elizabeth Glaser (AIDS awareness), Rosa Parks (civil rights), Alvin Sykes (social justice), medical and health professionals and the people they serve, and supporters of the Violence Against Women Act. Humble yet powerful, these folks and multitudes of others have forever influenced our nation and the wider world.

Imagine, Visualize, and Commit: Rosa Parks Assembles a Winning Team

"Stand for something or you will fall for anything. Today's mighty oak is yesterday's nut that held its ground." — Rosa Parks

Power Point ⇨ Aligned Connections

What's a strategic relationship, anyway? While Rosa Parks brought definite star power to the cause of teaching youth nonviolence techniques in America's schools, joining with individuals and groups who shared her passion was an important tactic in getting her message heard (and funded) on Capitol Hill. Parks' strategic connection to grassroots and national organizations aligned nicely with federal goals and attracted the interest of congressional leaders and the US Department of Education, which resulted in federal earmarked funding for her organization.

Imagination is the fuel of innovation and vision. It is daring and creative. Vision invites us to move forward boldly, steadfastly, and in alignment with a mind-set that helps others as well as ourselves. In *First Things First,* Stephen Covey writes,

> Vision is the best manifestation of creative imagination and the primary motivation of human action. It's the ability to see beyond our present reality, to create, to invent what does not yet exist, to become what we not yet are. It gives us capacity to live out of our imagination instead of our memory.

Most of us have heard about Rosa Parks, who became the mother of the civil rights movement on December 1, 1955, when she refused to move to the back of the bus in Montgomery, Alabama. I met Parks at the O Street Mansion in DC in the '90s. Invited to a cozy reception by Willis Edwards and Patricia Means, Parks needed a lobbyist, and I was honored to volunteer. Now, you may be asking yourself, "Why would Mrs. Parks need a lobbyist? She could meet with anyone she wanted." You are absolutely correct. Everybody in Washington, Republicans and Democrats, and particularly those in the Clinton administration, were more than happy to meet with her. Even with this access, she had difficulty securing federal help for her beloved nonprofit, the Rosa and Raymond Parks Institute, and its Pathways to Freedom program. I was engaged to help secure funding and strengthen strategic relationships. She needed earmarked funding and support for two programs targeting urban youth.

When Rosa Parks died in 2007, I received a call from Edwards and Elaine Steele, who asked me to serve as the congressional liaison to organize the historic placement of her body in the Capitol rotunda. We had four days. As a civilian, Parks would lie "in honor" (not "in state"), and she was the first African American woman and second African American to do so. The logistics were horrendous. Parks' body would be flown from Detroit to Montgomery, and then from Montgomery to Baltimore. Along the way, a special multijurisdictional police escort would accompany the caravan traveling with her body, family, dignitaries, and senior companions. Thankfully, folks stepped up, including US Representatives John Conyers and Eleanor Holmes Norton and former congresspersons, Jesse Jackson, Jr., and Carolyn Cheeks Kilpatrick, Donna Brazile, Leah Daugherty, Minyon Moore, and Hilary Shelton of the NAACP; House and Senate leadership team members; the Capitol police; and the DC Color Guard. Plus, the Washington Metropolitan Area Transportation Agency loaned a look-alike of the bus that sparked the historical Montgomery bus boycott. Also helping were Maryland state troopers, DC police, the pastor and members of the historic Metropolitan AME Church, and so many more.

Installation Ceremony for Parks' Statue in Statuary Hall of the US Capitol

President Barack Obama

President Obama and congressional leaders
unveiling the statue

Author with US Attorney General
Eric Holder

Author, Anita Estell, with Parks' friend and
confidant, Elaine Steele, in front of Parks' statue

Years later, on February 4, 2010, I was invited to celebrate Parks' ninety-seventh birthday in the Mansfield Room of the US Senate, just outside of the majority leader's office. A contingency of leaders attended (Majority Leader Harry Reid, Sens. Debbie Stabenow and Roland Burris, and Reps. John Conyers, Carolyn Kilpatrick, and Jesse Jackson Jr.). In addition to the many honors given to Parks (Congressional Gold Medal, Presidential Medal of Freedom, etc.), legislation was enacted commissioning a statue in her honor, which would be permanently placed in Statuary Hall, making her the first and only African American woman to be so honored. Parks' statue was installed in the US Capitol on February 27, 2013; leadership teams from the US House and Senate, President Obama, Steele and several hundred invited guests attended the installation ceremony. Parks' statue faces the statue of Robert E. Lee, a hero of the Confederacy. Almost two years prior to the installation of her statue at the US Capitol, in the spring of 2011, the Washington National Cathedral installed two stone carvings depicting Rosa Parks and Mother Teresa. The carvings are in the cathedral's Human Rights Porch. The cathedral reports that the carvings in this section "celebrate those who struggle to bring equality and social justice to all people."

Even with all of this, Parks was a woman of modest means whose strongest passion had everything to do with an abiding faith in God and in teaching young people how to exhibit strength without violence, the power of yielding without backing down, how to love without having to be loved back, and ultimately how to take a stand, even when sitting down.

Know the Issue: Alvin Sykes Settles Old Scores

Alvin Sykes, born in a home for unwed mothers when his mom was only fourteen, is an unlikely trailblazer. Taken in by a family friend, he suffered from epilepsy and grew up sickly.

To make matters worse, he reported being sexually abused by neighbors around age eleven. Sykes encountered his biological mother years later when he was homeless and they lived at the same shelter. His formal education was spotty: Sykes spent three years at Boys Town, the facility for at-risk kids in Omaha, and dropped out of school at sixteen.

Self-educated and driven, Sykes spent his days in a library and nights managing a band. He also sat in on trials to study legal tactics and researched what he didn't

---

Power Point ⇨ Education in Context

Napoleon Hill observes in *Think and Grow Rich* that some confuse the meaning of schooling and education. Hill writes, "The word *[education]* is derived from the Latin word *educo*, meaning to *educe*, to draw out, to develop from within." An educated person "is not, necessarily, one who has an abundance of general or specialized knowledge. An educated [person] is one who has so developed the faculties of his mind that he may acquire anything he wants, or its equivalent, without violating the rights of others."

> ### Power Point ⇨ Try This
> Read the Till Act in part or in full at govtrack.us. See who sponsored the bill and which way the votes went.

understand. In 2008, Senator Tom Coburn had an article from the Atlanta-Constitution, written by Drew Jubera, profiling Sykes reprinted in the *Congressional Record*. In that reprint, Sykes is quoted: "Education was important to me, that's the reason I left school. The administration was more concerned with students getting a piece of paper than an education. So I started teaching myself." Sykes had worked for or founded a variety of local victims' rights groups, rarely living on more than ten thousand dollars a year. In 2003, he read that Emmett Till's mother wanted her son's case reopened. Emmett was fourteen in 1955 when he was brutally murdered in Money, Mississippi, where he was spending summer vacation. The Chicago teen was accused of whistling at a white woman, and for that, he was bludgeoned and battered. His mother, Mamie Till-Mobley, threw fuel on the fire of the civil rights movement when she made the brave decision to leave Emmett's casket open for his funeral.

In 2003, Sykes and Till-Mobley founded the Emmett Till Justice Campaign. Till-Mobley died shortly after and Sykes pressed on, brokering meetings with senators, district attorneys, and victims' relatives to seek long-delayed justice and the eventual FBI reinvestigation. During that investigation, however, Sykes learned of many other unresolved cases from that era. While the FBI's renewed inquiry on Till returned no indictment, Sykes helped draft and introduce the Emmett Till Unsolved Civil Rights Crime Act. The measure was signed into law by President George W. Bush in 2008 and established a unit in the US Department of Justice to investigate the era's unsolved murders. The measure received bipartisan sponsorship, with Representatives John Lewis (D-GA) and Kenny Hulshof (R-MO) taking the lead.

Plug into the Source and FLOW: A Profoundly Personal and Life-Changing Story

In the fall of 2011, I lost speech, memory, and strength on my right side. My handwriting changed. My vision blurred. I thought I had had a stroke. As the symptoms quickly worsened, I hustled to my primary care physician to obtain a referral for a neurologist. Two days later, an MRI confirmed the presence of a cystic mass (tumor) in my brain the size of a plum or small orange. With the assistance of a friend, in less than three days, I was able to secure a meeting with the head of the Johns Hopkins tumor program, a neurosurgeon by the name of Dr. Alfredo Quinones-Hinojosa (Dr. Q). The interesting thing about Dr. Q is that he came to the United States as an illegal migrant worker, lived in a trailer (propped on bricks) that should have been on the bed of a truck, and eventually worked his way from community college to the University of California, Berkeley, and then on to Harvard Medical School. True story.

During our initial consultation, he began by saying that while he was recognized as one of the best surgeons in his field, what would take place in the operating room was much more profound than the skills of his hands. He referenced God and noted the importance of the energy of his team and me, the patient, being in alignment and working in synchronicity with the surgeon. It would *be* important for each of us to be plugged into each other and that omnipotent, omnipresent Source that is bigger than all of us but available to each of us.

We met on Wednesday, and the surgery was scheduled for the following Monday. I had two business days to get my professional and medical affairs together. I climbed onto the surgical table at noon on Monday. The procedure took five hours. Dr. Q was assisted by an incredible health and medical team at Johns Hopkins Bayview Hospital. They sliced my scalp, cracked my skull, pierced my brain, and popped the cystic sac that contained twenty cubic centimeters (about half a cup) of fluid and peeled the tumor from the frontal lobe of my brain like it was an onion or piece of fruit—all without shaving any of my hair. I awakened from anesthesia talking, ecstatic about what seemed like a miracle to me in that (1) I was alive, (2) humans have the talents to invent the technology and perform all the steps associated with the surgery, and (3) all the limitations I had prior to surgery were gone. Vanished. Poof. The fact that I could speak and remember again so quickly had me talking a mile a minute. Folks literally asked me to shut up. The very next day, I fed myself breakfast, lunch, and dinner. After receiving the approval of the occupational and physical therapists, I was released to go home by 10:00 a.m. on Wednesday, less than forty-eight hours after the surgery. Amazing. I had no physical limitations or disabilities.

Once home, for the first two days, I heard the song "Amazing Grace" playing as if it had been piped into an invisible field that surrounded me. The words "I was blind but now I see . . . it was Grace . . . that saved a wretch like me" took on a new meaning. Grace. Yes. Grace used what could have been a traumatic episode to make itself known to me—transfusing my faith and transforming my life profoundly. And, just to make sure I truly understood, I received affirmation repeatedly. I listened to an audio book with a chapter on "Amazing Grace." I watched *Jeopardy*, and one of the answers was "Amazing Grace." After a while, I stilled myself and listened. I also felt what I describe as the wings of angels and felt a sense of protection and comfort that was more profound than joy. And, no, it was not the oxycodone. It was an energy force that made itself

Power Point ⇨ Speaking Truth to Power

What I learned during my recovery was this: Life is our invitation and opportunity to serve as evidence of God's magnificence and majesty. We are tenants and thus have a responsibility to the Landlord. Our security deposits for the lives we have been given and the bodies we occupy are the pursuit of excellence and good health. The rent we pay (borrowing in part from Marian Wright Edelman) is loving and helping others. All else is either vanity or evil. Vanity is obsessive self-love and evil is the absence of love.

known so that I would share this story, this testimony, with you and so that I would always know that there is a Power that not only takes care of the flowers in the field but that also takes care of each of us.

During my two-week follow-up visit, Dr. Q confirmed that the tumor was a benign grade 1 meningioma. The causal factors are not clearly understood. I count my blessings still today.

Ironically, the cynic in me thought, if this issue had been left in the hands of elected officials, the surgery might have been delayed until after an election, and rather than moving as a team with the care of the patient having top priority, the surgeons may have left the patient to suffer as those paid to provide a vital service argued over whether to use staples or sutures to close a bleeding wound. On the other hand, I had a deeper appreciation for the work I have done in the private sector and as a Capitol Hill staffer in helping members of Congress and others fund biomedical research programs at the National Institutes of Health, and I realized that I was a beneficiary of that investment. I give thanks.

Coalesce, Communicate, and Engage: Violence Against Women Act of 1994 Establishes Accountability

In 1983, Tracey Thurman, twenty-two, was brutally stabbed thirteen times and suffered a broken neck at the hands of her estranged husband. Some of the injuries occurred after a Torrington, Connecticut police officer arrived. Thurman lay helpless as her husband wandered about unrestrained, kicking her twice in the head as she bled. This man ultimately dropped their two-year son on her bloody torso. The case received national media coverage. *Thurman v. Torrington* became the first federal case in which a battered woman sued a city for the failure of police to protect her from spousal violence. Thurman eventually won a two-million-dollar judgment against the city for its inaction and the scars and partial paralysis caused by the beating. Over the next decade, this case and the issue of domestic violence galvanized a broad-based coalition of national and local women's organizations, other stakeholders, and a bipartisan group of political leaders. Today, several national organizations, including the American Association of University Women, Legal Momentum, the National Organization for Women, the National Network to End Domestic Violence, and YWCA USA, participate as a coalition in efforts related to this issue.

According to the US Department of Justice, a quarter to a third of women experience domestic violence in their lifetimes. Data collection, education, advocacy, service delivery, and investigations and arrests of perpetrators all have improved following the enactment of the Violence Against Women Act of 1994 (VAWA). This is one of few federal laws that engage policymakers, advocates, and nonprofits at the national, state, county, and local levels and within tribal communities. In 2009, President Barack Obama and Vice President Joseph Biden announced the historic

Power Point ⇨ More Examples of Effective Coalitions

Another example of the power of coalitions: A coalition representing a group of historically black colleges and universities and other minority institutions of higher education flexed its muscle in 2010, securing 2.5 billion dollars in mandatory funding over a ten-year period. The funding was included in a provision accompanying the controversial health care law enacted that year—Affordable Care Act.

appointment of a White House advisor (Lynn Rosenthal) on the issue. In addition to leading efforts related to VAWA, the person holding this position is responsible for coordinating interagency collaboration; implementing victim assistance programs; and integrating these issues into administration-wide programs, such as the White House Fatherhood Initiative, the White House Council on Women and Girls, HUD's fight against homelessness, and the Justice Department's recent effort to better combat disproportionate violence in tribal communities. In 2013, as a result of efforts spearheaded by Representative Gwen Moore (D-WI), VAWA was expanded and reauthorized as a matter of law.

Persevere and Lay a Foundation: Elizabeth Glaser Makes AIDS Efforts a Matter of Life and Death

I didn't know much about Elizabeth Glaser before she launched an international advocacy effort on behalf of pediatric AIDS. I did know this issue had her sole, most passionate attention when I first met her. I recall vividly the day she paid a visit to the congressional office where I worked as the senior staffer responsible for House Labor-HHS-Education Appropriations Subcommittee programs. Slightly built, Glaser was armed with a compelling story and well-developed briefing materials needed to move the discussions along quickly. She seemed to have almost everything going for her: She had married well; her husband was Paul Michael Glaser of *Starsky and Hutch* fame. She had mothered a beautiful boy and a girl. She lived in sunny California. She had everything a woman could want except for time and the ability to access and develop an effective treatment for HIV/AIDS for herself and her children.

Glaser contracted HIV early in the AIDS epidemic after receiving an HIV-contaminated blood transfusion in 1981 while giving birth to her daughter, Ariel. Like many other HIV-infected mothers, Glaser unknowingly passed the virus to Ariel through breastfeeding. In 1984, she gave birth to a son, Jake, who had contracted HIV in the womb. The virus went undetected in all three until they underwent HIV testing in 1985. In these years, little was known about this disease, particularly mother-to-child transmission. Treatments for adults were in the experimental stages, and treatments for children were nonexistent. Glaser lost Ariel in 1988. Determined to help her son and other HIV-infected children, she cofounded the Elizabeth Glaser Pediatric AIDS Foundation in 1988. By the time I met Glaser, in 1990 or 1991, she aggressively sought assistance from federal policymakers, knowing that in her race to save her son's life, time was her enemy.

Power Point ⇨ PEPFAR Perseveres

Today, America can lay claim to one of the world's most effective efforts to combat HIV/AIDS globally. The cornerstone to President George W. Bush's Global Health Initiative, PEPFAR (President's Emergency Plan for AIDS Relief), has been widely praised for succeeding in its historic commitment to combating a single disease by committing billions of dollars and organizational leadership.

Glaser died in 1994.

The Elizabeth Glaser Pediatric AIDS Foundation is now the leading nonprofit dedicated to pediatric AIDS work around the world. Glaser's efforts have raised public awareness about HIV infection in children and spurred funding for the development of pediatric AIDS drugs as well as research into mother-to-child HIV transmission. Today, an entire community of pediatric AIDS research is under way where none existed before. Fewer children are born with HIV, and children with HIV infection live longer and healthier lives. In every relevant area of the federal government—from research priorities at the National Institutes of Health to Congress—children with HIV are a focus of targeted interest and resources. While Glaser lost her personal battle with AIDS, Jake has lived to be an adult and is actively engaged with his mother's legacy effort, which benefits millions of children around the world.

This is what it looks like when we put the power equation, power line and power characteristics together.

VISION x	KNOWLEDGE x	POWER x (FLOW or FLOP)	n(PEACE)	= Change
Discover ➡	Develop ➡	Innovate ➡	Aggregate ➡	Sustain & Scale
Imagine, Visualize & Commit	Know the Issue & Plan	Plug into the Source and FLOW	Coalesce, Communicate & Engage	Persevere & Lay a Foundation

CHAPTER 4

Be the Dream

D o you believe you can influence policymakers and the decisions they make? If you could change five things about America, what would they be? If you could influence the present, what would you do? How about the future; what would you ask elected officials to do to help your family, community, and the world? What are your thoughts about the national debt? What can Congress do to help create good jobs that pay well? Take a moment before you answer these questions. Think. Write your answers on a piece of paper. Put them in a safe place to retrieve later.

The reverberations of decisions and discussions being made now at the national level will affect state and local governments, businesses, communities, and individuals for many years to come. We have come to a fork in the road. The choices we make and path we choose now—collectively as citizens—will take us closer to annihilation or down a path of extraordinary discovery of our true potential as human beings.

In 2011, the world as I knew it shifted dramatically. Confidence in America emerged as the central issue needing resuscitation. For the first time in our nation's history, questions about the nation's credit rating, the markets, and most notably the confidence of consumers shaped discussions for many months. Uncertainty emerged as a parallel theme. The democratic process seemed threatened by disruptions related to debt discussions and the absence of relevant leadership. There actually were times when I thought about walking away from it all. Ultimately, the absence of approaches, efforts, mechanisms, and consensus needed to resolve some of the most troubling issues of my lifetime and potentially this century prompted a profound rediscovery of some basic truths. I recalled how, when I was a little girl, my mother would say, "Where there is a will, there is a way" and "What goes around comes around." Even as a child, I accepted these threads of guidance as universal natural laws. Now that I am older, I realize that the will *is* the way. Thought is an actual working power. Even Jesus acknowledged this when he said, "It is done unto you as you believe," and when he directed us to "Do unto others as you would have them do unto you."

Cause and Effect: Deficit Thinking

Soon, I realized that there is no point in worrying about the dysfunctionality of Capitol Hill or the world, for that matter. Lessons first introduced to me as a young adult bellowed: "If we as a community of players want to change the world, we must change the way we see and think about the world—and each other. When we change our thoughts, we change the way we engage, thus changing the cause, which changes the effect." In this light, and as noted by David R. Hawkins in *Power vs. Force*, the objective and subjective are one and the same, not even two different sides of the same coin—the same.

From quantum physics, we know that the impulses and information we define as energy are in everything. In his book *Creating Affluence: The A to Z Steps to a Richer Life*, Deepak Chopra notes that "those same impulses of energy and information that we experience as thoughts—those same impulses—are the raw material of the universe. . . . [A]t a preverbal level, all nature speaks the same language. We are all thinking bodies in a thinking universe. And just as thought projects itself as the molecules of our body, so too the same impulses of energy and information project themselves as space-time events in our environment."

Take the national debt issue, for example. The alarms sounded as America approached the August 2, 2011, deadline to increase the nation's debt ceiling. The alarms sounded not because we were in a real crisis but because we had a group of national leaders who had difficulty reaching an agreement. In October 2013, alarms sounded again with a 17-day shutdown of the federal government and a toxic partisan stalemate that pushed our country to the brink of a possible default on our national debt and also threatened to exhaust our borrowing authority. Ultimately, a last-minute deal was reached to reopen the government and to extend the limits on US borrowing authority. The shutdown resembled a fool's errand in that it cost taxpayers about $24 billion. In both instances, in 2011 and 2013, leadership and vision were offered as sacrifices on the altar of political expediency.

The role of government has looked more like a drama than service to the people. The Republicans and Democrats would have us believe they are, at their core, very different kinds of people (possibly from different planets), and they labor daily (and spend billions of dollars) to convince the masses that that is so. Bizarre and unnatural contortions are required to defend and protect this illusion. The consequences for those they have been elected to serve have been particularly acute.

At a most basic level, consider those cities, communities, and states that have members of Congress from both parties. I have personally witnessed on several occasions how these officials' allegiance to competing parties actually prevents them

---

Power Point ⇨ No Thumbs Up for National Leaders

Most agree that something is seriously wrong with Washington, DC. Several polls, including a 2010 Mc-Clatchy-Ipsos poll, show an estimated 80 percent of Americans think the federal government is broken. Another significant percentage are pessimistic and unengaged.

Power Point ⇨ Growing Income Inequality

Filmmaker Michael Moore reports on his website that in 2009, the bottom 60 percent of US households owned only 2.3 percent of total US wealth, just 1.22 trillion dollars of the country's approximately 53 trillion dollars. This amount is less than the estimated combined net worth of those people listed on Forbes 400. How could it be that only *400* people in the United States have more wealth than half of the more than *100 million* US households? Is it reasonable that the recession of 2009 devastated many wage earners and small businesses but the net worth of the Forbes 400 jumped to 1.37 trillion dollars in 2010?

from actively coordinating their efforts to work together for the benefit of the very community that elected them. Even the folks at Harvard are concerned by this state of affairs. In an article appearing in the *Harvard Business Review*, Harvard School of Business Professor David Moss writes,

> What's different now has less to do with how America's politicians campaign than how they govern. Voting in Congress is the most polarized it has been in well over a hundred years. . . . The phenomenon seems to have taken on a life of its own, and it is threatening the nation's capacity to solve critical problems, from employment to energy to entitlements to education.

Truth is, America is not running out of money. We had and have plenty of money and natural resources and enough *potential* talent and ingenuity to drive the innovations we need for many years to come. So, what's the problem? Perception and political gridlock top the list. Cut through the clutter and you will see there really is no problem we cannot overcome, that is, *if* we change the way we think and move quickly to *effectively* address where we are now. If we keep on thinking America is broke, it will be. Moreover, the more profound answers and solutions lie in the choices we make to hold ourselves and those we elect to office accountable.

Did you know?

While the United States is not considered the wealthiest country in the world (Qatar holds that distinction), it does have the largest economy (14.99 trillion dollars)—double that of China (7.3 trillion dollars)—according to 2012 information published by the World Bank.

Power Point ⇨ New Measures of Success

The United Nation's Human Development Index measures three quality of life areas: health and longevity, knowledge, and income. Under the HDI, the United States ranks fourth, but on the UN "inequality adjusted" index, it ranks twenty-third. Consider also the country of Bhutan, which uses a gross national happiness index. (*See* Justin Fox, "The Economics of Well-Being," *Harvard Business Review*, January-February 2012, pages 82-83: "Many things of value in life cannot be captured by GDP, but they can be measured by metrics of health, education and freedom.")

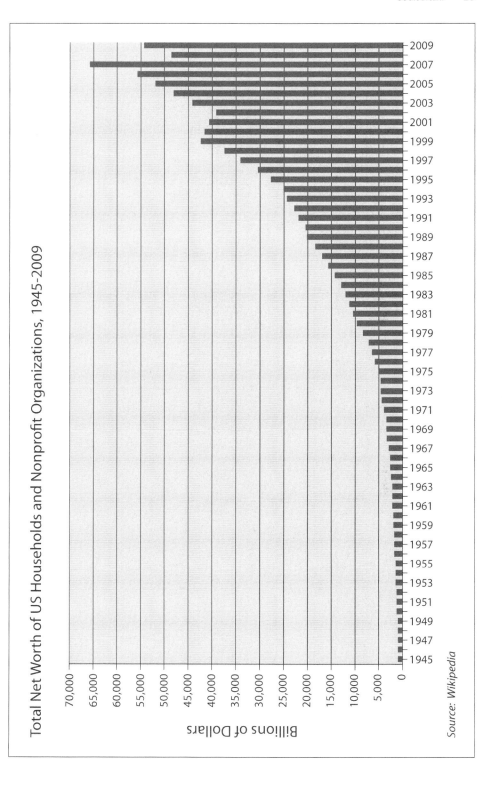

Total Net Worth of US Households and Nonprofit Organizations, 1945-2009

Billions of Dollars

Source: Wikipedia

> ### Power Point ⇨ Liquid Substance
> Water constitutes 80 percent of the earth's surface. It also makes up 60-80 percent of human body mass. Eighty-five percent of the brain is water. In nature, water can take the form of a gas, liquid, or solid. Without water, there would be no life as we know it.

We Perceive; Therefore It Is and Is Not

The facts speak for themselves. Or do they? It depends on your perception.

Perception is basically a process by which people choose to see the world around them a certain way. We often mistake our perceptions for reality, allowing them to guide our behavior. Our sensory experiences lead to artificial perceptual constructs created in the imagination.

An example used often in American culture and politics involves a half glass of water. Depending on one's perception, the glass is either half empty or half full. It really doesn't matter who is right or who is wrong. The reality is, it's just a half glass of water. Within a political context, what *matters* most is what you *imagine* you can do with what you have been given, and what you do with it in your imagination is influenced by your attitudes, beliefs, knowledge, values, and level of conscious awareness.

Take that partial glass of water. At one level of awareness, its source—a river, lake, or ocean—is seen as a place to dispose of waste. At another level, in places like drought-stricken parts of the world, water is a vital resource—access to which affects the fate of nations and peoples. It is the original thirst quencher. It can also be used to help and heal when taking a pill or cleaning a wound. Half a glass of water when used appropriately in a laboratory experiment can unlock a discovery related to a cure for a disease or other relevant research. At a spiritual level, water can symbolize transformation and transcendence. Recall the story of Jesus Christ walking on water or the miracle he performed for his mother (Mary) when she asked him to turn water into wine. The next time you see a half glass of water, imagine what it represents to you . . . and what you can do with it.

The Golden Rule

Making decisions built on wisdom, justice, compassion, and respect for our shared status as neighbors is always the most important objective. This principle is established in religions around the world and in science. We are familiar with the scripture "love thy neighbor as thyself," one of two commandments Jesus shared in the New Testament. Consider *ubuntu*, a Zulu and Bantu term meaning "I am who I am because of who you are." Bishop Desmond Tutu describes the philosophy in this way:

> One of the sayings in our country is Ubuntu—the essence of being human. Ubuntu speaks particularly about the fact that you can't exist as a human

Power Point ⇨ Ubuntu American Style

Ambassador Elizabeth Frawley Bagley was sworn in as the Department of State's first Special Representative for Global Partnerships. In her swearing-in remarks, Ambassador Bagley described "*Ubuntu Diplomacy*: where all sectors belong as partners, where we all participate as stakeholders, and where we all succeed together, not incrementally but exponentially." (US Department of State, Press Release, June 23, 2009)

being in isolation. It speaks about our interconnectedness. You can't be human all by yourself, and when you have this quality—Ubuntu—you are known for your generosity.

We think of ourselves far too frequently as just individuals, separated from one another, whereas you are connected and what you do affects the whole World. When you do well, it spreads out; it is for the whole of humanity. *Retrieved from Wikipedia, January 15, 2012.*

This Golden Rule theme appears in many cultures and religions. In Sanskrit, the word *namaste* (pronounced nah-may-STAY) means "the spirit in me honors the spirit in you." In Tibetan Buddhism, living with an open heart by practicing *Tonglen* and having an enlightened heart *bodhicitta* dissolve the barriers that separate us. These barriers often emanate from fear and present themselves as greed, hatred and misperception.

Theoretical physics also confirms what the sages know and knew to be true. Dr. David Hawkins offers this:

The Universe holds its breath as we choose, instant by instant, which pathway to follow. . . . Every act, thought, and choice adds to a permanent mosaic; our decisions ripple through the universe of consciousness to affect the lives of all. . . . [L]et's remember that fundamental tenet of the new theoretical physics: Everything in the universe is connected to everything else.

He also adds this:

Our choices reinforce the formation of powerful M-Fields, which are the attractor patterns that influence others whether we wish them to or not. Every act or decision we make that supports life supports all life, including

Power Point ⇨ Mother's Wit

Even my mother used to say, "What goes around, comes around; if you don't do good, good don't follow."

Also, the Gaia hypothesis, named after the Greek goddess of the earth, "affirms a view based on scientific reasoning that was, in essence, also held by all traditional cultures and peoples, a world in which humans were interconnected and interdependent with all beings and with the earth itself" (Jon Kabat-Zinn, *Full Catastrophe Living*).

our own. The ripples we create return to us—this, which may have seemed a metaphysical statement, is now established as scientific fact.

In this sphere of ultimate accountability, it is refreshing to see the intersection of scientific findings, ancient truths, scriptures and teachings embraced for thousands of years by diverse peoples around the world.

CHAPTER 5
The Original Power Tools:
Body, Mind, Spirit, Soul, and Unity of Purpose

When I started to write this chapter, I focused on the tools needed to master the process of gaining access and getting certain results from the federal government: how to get a meeting with a member of Congress, what to say when you get there, and so on. But that approach didn't feel right for this part of the book. I said a prayer and requested an answer to my quandary. And somewhere in the wee hours of the morning, it hit me. An inner voice provided the guidance I needed.

Aware, informed, well-intentioned, compassionate, and healthy people can transform communities, governments, and nations when they are properly organized and engaged. Human beings are naturally equipped with what we need to sculpt our individual and collective destiny—in an extraordinary way. We come into the world wired for consciousness and equipped with a survival kit and power pack: our minds, bodies, spirits and souls. We are most powerful when these fields of energy work together and in collaboration with the creative force that accompanies us for the greater good.

In his State of the Union Address on January 6, 1941, Franklin D. Roosevelt had this to say about the power of the hands, hearts, and minds of free men and women:

> This nation has placed its destiny in the hands and heads and hearts of its millions of free men and women, and its faith in freedom under the guidance of God. Freedom means the supremacy of human rights everywhere. Our support goes to those who struggle to gain those rights and keep them. Our strength is our unity of purpose.

The ten-thousand-mile journey toward freedom begins with a first step pointed toward unity of purpose. Individually and collectively, we share a responsibility for the welfare of all people and the planet. We essentially are tools in God's toolbox. Everyday decisions are connected to a unified field of infinite possibilities, a reciprocal arrangement called life. It is our nature to engage and connect as individuals and communities. Each of us has a distinct purpose and contribution to make. Our fingerprints and DNA confirm our uniqueness. In understanding our purpose, the first step is to look within to understand who we are as well as those things that are the objects of our attention.

Recall the story about two boys who enjoyed taunting an old woman who lived on the beach. One day, they found a young bird and decided they wanted to trick that lady. The scheme was as follows: One boy said to the other, "Let's play a trick on the ol' lady. We have this bird. We are going to approach the ol' lady, show her the bird, and then I am going to put my hands behind my back. We will ask her which hand holds the tiny bird, the left or the right? We are going to tell her that if she chooses the hand with the bird, the bird will be crushed to death. But, here's the kicker." The boy leaned over to shield his trickery and whispered, "The bird will surely die. If the ol' lady picks the hand of liberation, I am going to switch hands. If she picks the hand that causes suffering, then so it will be."

The two boys ran to the ol' lady's house and knocked on her door. She opened the door and stepped outside. The mastermind of the plot launched into the dastardly scheme.

"Ol' lady," he said, "you see, I have this bird. You have the power to determine if it lives or dies. Tell you what I'm gonna do. I'm gonna clench this bird in one of my hands after placing both hands behind my back. I'm gonna ask you to pick a hand, and if you choose the hand with the bird, I'm gonna crush this little baby bird to death!" The ol' lady sighed and shook her head. The young fella commanded her, "Now pick a hand." The ol' lady took a moment, assessed the situation, and then said, "I cannot say. You see, whether that little bird actually lives or dies is in your hands—It is in your hands."

The story is a metaphor for the choice of liberation or suffering we face each day. Before the little boy decided to tighten or loosen his grip, he would have to look within himself and scan his heart, mind, spirit and soul to decide what to do with his hands. The outcome would be determined by his level of awareness, his respect for life, whether he removed his ego from the decision-making process, and what he actually chooses to do with his hands.

While federal laws and regulations touch almost every aspect of our lives, and may even be applicable to the scenario involving the bird above, the reality is that the state of affairs in the US and on the planet is in our hands – as individuals and citizens. The nature of our laws and condition of our world have everything to do with how we exercise our freedom and creativity, including the choices we make in pursuing our passions and how we treat each other and other living things on the planet.

Like the little boy above, our thought processes are inextricably linked to who we are and what we do. The human body functions through the synchronization of one hundred trillion cells. It is a miniature universe of activity in itself that demands balance.

Whole industries and government sectors have multibillion-dollar enterprises that do nothing but assess our level of awareness, needs, wants, fears, thoughts, feelings, and behaviors. In many respects, the government and big corporations know more about us than we know about ourselves. Mindful and enlightened citizen engagement means purposeful movement from the inside looking out. Remember what FDR said: with God's guidance and through the use of our hands, hearts, and minds, "our ultimate strength is derived from our unity of purpose."

Energy Zone	Translation	Looks/Feels Like	Optimum State
Awareness/ Spirit/Soul	I am	Being, presence, Bigger than life	Freedom/Power
Heart	I feel	Emotions, feelings	Love
Brain/Mind	I think	Thoughts, knowledge, attention & intention	Wisdom
Whole Body	I do	Behavior	Justice/Balance

Basic human states involve, first, just being—as in human being—and then feeling, thinking, and doing, which work together as a whole field of energy most commonly known as the human body. Moving through life, being human looks something like this: I am. I feel. I think. I do. Enlightened citizenship and collective action invite a deeper understanding of our essence and relevance.

Awareness/Consciousness/Spirit/Soul

The essence of being human extends beyond the rational mind. Science, religion, and indigenous studies enlisting different approaches end up in the same place—that there are physical and nonphysical characteristics associated with *being human*. Varying terms are used to describe this phenomenon: awareness, consciousness, soul, spirit, nonlocal, unmanifested, and others. It is a domain that exists beyond time and space. Sometimes the words *soul* and *spirit* are used interchangeably, and sometimes they are not. Whatever the case, there is that essence of who we are that can manifest as the knower, the observer, an inner voice that appears independent of thought. It is that place where purpose, creativity, insight, and intuition reside. It serves as the link to a power bigger than us but that connects each of us to a field of infinite possibilities.

The roots of the word *soul* can be traced back to the Hebrew word *ne'phesh* and the Greek word *psy-khe'*. These words are not necessarily identical in meaning, but they refer to living creatures—people, animals, or the life of a person or animal. Genesis 2:7 instructs, "The Lord God formed man of the dust of the ground, and breathed into his

Power Point ⇨ Genesis 2:7

The formula given in Genesis 2:7 is not man equals body plus soul; the formula there is soul equals dust plus breath. According to this verse, God did not make a body and put a soul into it, like a letter into an envelope. He formed man of dust; then, by breathing His breath into it, He made the dust live. The dust, formed as man and made to live, did not embody a soul, it became a soul-that is, a whole creature. Humanity is thus presented to us, in Adam, not as a creature of two discrete parts temporarily glued together but as a single mystery.

(Wikipedia, s.v. "*Soul in the Bible*," retrieved January 15, 2013, Note 7, Wendell Berry (1997) "*Christianity and the Survival of Creation*")

nostrils the breath of life; and man became a living soul." Compare this to the comments related to the word *spirit* that follow.

The origins of the word *spirit* can be traced back to the Hebrew word *ru'ach* and the Greek work *pneu'ma*. In Hebrew, it means "breath" or "wind," and in Greek, it also means "air in motion." Spirit, then, is that spark, or invisible life force, that animates humans and other living creatures. In some religions, spirit refers to an active force associated with the word *holy*, as in Holy Spirit. Mother Teresa once said that "holiness is not a luxury for the few; it is simply a duty, for you and for me."

The Heart

Author Gary Zukav, in his book *The Seat of the Soul*, says, "[T]he way to your soul is through your heart." Proverbs 4:23 states, "More than all else that is to be guarded, safeguard your heart, for out of it are the sources of life." Physicians and spiritual teachers say the heart is the master oscillator of the body. The human heart emits an electromagnetic field that surrounds the entire body. This field sends signals to every cell in the body, affecting physical, mental, and emotional health and well-being. In politics as in life, it is best to move with a loving and compassionate heart.

Power Point ⇨ Illiteracy and the Heart

Note also the observation by Aristotle that "educating the mind without educating the heart is no education at all."

Brain and Mind

The human brain has been compared to a computer that is far more advanced than the most elaborate artificial intelligence machine. Once we give something our attention, mental events transform themselves as molecules, science reveals. These messenger molecules, known as *neuropeptides*, are connectors and carriers of thought, and they permeate every cell of the body. We also know that the brain is not a fixed anatomical structure; it has a plasticity (plastic-like quality) that allows it to change, grow, heal or fixate. It embodies a collection of processes that influence (and are influenced by) the flow of energy and information within us, between us and around us.

Consider the poem by Emily Dickinson about the brain in which she states that the brain is wider than the sky and deeper than the ocean because one contains the other.

Brain and mind are also that place wherein wisdom resides. Power without wisdom is for the foolish at best and the wicked at worst.

Power Point ⇨ Wisdom

How one defines wisdom makes all the difference. Consider the definition from Romans 3:15-18, which states that the most powerful type of wisdom is neither jealous nor contentious. It "is chaste, then peaceable, reasonable, ready to obey, full of mercy and good fruits, not making partial distinction, not hypocritical."

The Whole Body

Beyond the brain and heart, other parts of the human anatomy and physiology are vital to the proper functioning of the whole body as absorber, conductor, and emitter of energy. Every element of our being has a distinctly defined role but all have one objective: to support the proper functioning of the whole body. It is more than a coincidence that discussions related to health care, obesity, nutrition, exercise, and addiction are receiving so much attention at the national level as a matter of public policy. Sure, escalating health care costs and the need to provide more affordable, quality care options are contributing factors. But a growing number of people are aware of how healthy mind-sets and habits contribute to the quality of life. There is a wondrous intricacy and complexity to being human. We truly are designed to connect beyond ourselves. It is through the alignment of our thoughts, words, and deeds and our minds, bodies, spirits and souls that we exhibit talents and abilities to create the tools and approaches that influence and manipulate the world in which we live.

Unity of Purpose and the Substance of Renewal

Recall the quote, "Let them eat cake"? The irony inherent in this quote is that there would be no cake, or for our purposes, there would be no nations, but for the efforts of the people. More important, to be strong and vibrant, people and nations need more than cake; strong and healthy nations need strong and healthy people. They need sustenance that nourishes minds, strengthens limbs, builds muscles, and soothes souls. In most nations, including the United States, the people are the farmers who harvest the grains and manufacture the ingredients needed to make this food. They are the owners of the intellectual property and inventions that make product manufacturing and distribution possible. They are the factory workers who assemble the appliances needed for baking and warehouses for storing. They staff the distribution and delivery channels and drive the vehicles that take the final product to market. They are the entrepreneurs who convert sales into profit. They are the taxpayers who shoulder the financial burdens associated with hard work. They are the security forces willing to place their lives on the line when faced with an outside threat. They are the private citizens who opt for public service as elected officials. They are the folks who lick the bowl and put their finger in the mix every time they show up to vote and provide their consent to be governed, knowing they are taking a chance that those they elect may not get it right. They are the greedy fat cats who have confused overeating with success and who stumble about dazed on a post-binging high. They are the hungry and the poor who consider government-subsidized crumbs a feast. They are the cleanup crew when it all falls apart. They are the master chefs who delight in trying to do better next time. Their struggle and sacrifice (fortified by blood, sweat, and tears) form the iron caste needed for baking. The substance of renewal, their hopes, dreams, and intentions rise time and again, signaling the surrender and defeat of impossibility.

CHAPTER 6

Get Started: Frame Your Vision Exercise

Before you jump into freedom's waters, there are a few things you should ask yourself and know how to do. Making a real difference in your community or your nation requires more than having a good idea or hoping for the best. It requires having a clear vision and devising a plan that can be implemented.

Below, please find a vision exercise intended to set the tone for the next section, which includes the information and resource guide. Please complete the exercise to the best of your ability. If you are unable to complete the exercise at this time, no worries. Just proceed to the next section. After reading the information and resource guide materials, please take a stab at completing the exercise.

Frame Your Vision: "Be the dream" Exercise

You were asked to answer several questions at the beginning of chapter 4 and to save your answers in a safe place until later. Please retrieve those answers, which you may find helpful, but are not necessary for this exercise. This exercise is intended to help you embrace and focus your power.

Using the answers you developed previously, or by creating new answers, list fifteen things that you like about the United States. Begin the sentence with "What I really love about the United States is . . ."

Using the answers above, or by creating new responses, make a list of up to fifteen issues or concerns that you are passionate about and would like to change at the national or local levels of government. Be sure to take your time and really think about those issues that are most significant and important to you and that arouse your most passionate convictions. Begin the sentence with "What I have a passion for and would love to change and make better in the United States is . . ."

Now, select fifteen words from the first list and one word from each sentence, up to fifteen words, from the second list that capture your attention or jump out at you. These are known as power or energy words. You should have at most thirty words, with a maximum of fifteen words from each list.

Take these power or energy words and write a paragraph, poem, song, or other piece about what you most desire to see as a reality in the United States or in America's relationships with other parts of the world.

Once you complete this exercise, you are ready to move to the next section of the handbook.

SECTION TWO

Information and Resources for Persons
of Passion and Vision

CHAPTER 7

The Art of Advocacy: Translating Thoughts, Words, and Deeds Into Tangible Results

Soup is running free in the street—if only I had a spoon. — Aunt Charlene

The first part of this handbook discussed the relevance of aligning thoughts, words, and deeds and the role the power equation plays in enlightened citizen engagement. This part of the book provides a rubber-meets-the-road or a teach-a-person-to-fish discussion on what it takes to achieve enduring results in Washington. You may find it useful to keep your answers from the vision exercise at the end of the previous section handy as you read the discussion that follows.

This part of the book extends the conversation from enlightenment to effective and exemplary engagement and collective action. It addresses how the federal government works and how to get it to work for you. Simply stated, it's all about effective advocacy. Definitions of advocacy, tactics, techniques, timelines, and tools that inform communications, outreach, and strategy are given here. Charts and other graphics simplify the discussion. Earlier discussions related to the power equation, power characteristics, and power line are synthesized and connected to other critical components that drive impact and change.

First Things First: What Is Advocacy?

There are numerous manuals and resources about advocacy and related activities, and some of them are referenced within the bibliography located at the back of this book. Rather than offer you a step-by-step guide dissecting the nuances of what it takes to develop and implement an advocacy campaign, I have synthesized and distilled the most important, tangible elements I've learned from research and, more relevantly, twenty-plus years as a successful practitioner who has helped Americans across the nation design and implement strategies and plans with actual results. Some of those personal stories appeared in the first part of the book. For many causes I have been associated with, I have prayed, cried, perspired, lost sleep, and experienced the full continuum of highs and lows that come with hard-fought battles. I know firsthand that the information shared here actually works. It has worked for me and the people I have had the pleasure to know and represent. Many of the people with whom I have worked most directly have served those with small wallets—but with proactive minds and big hearts. Quantitatively, we are talking about efforts and results at the federal level valued in the billions of dollars, affecting the lives of millions. Qualitatively, the value of education, freedom, opportunity, and improved life conditions is immeasurable.

Advocacy: A Sister to Freedom

There are many definitions of advocacy. One set of definitions related to advocacy appears in a paper contracted by the US Agency for International Development, the agency that provides assistance to emerging democracies and developing and underdeveloped countries around the world. The paper, titled "Advocacy Strategies for Civil Society: A Conceptual Framework and Practitioner's Guide," published in 1997 by Leslie M. Fox and Priya Helweg, outlines three stages of advocacy. Each phase correlates to a stage on a continuum of advocacy strategy. They are (1) transformational (empowering citizens), (2) developmental (strengthening communities and societies), and (3) instrumental (influencing policy). What this essentially means is that different advocacy approaches serve people with different needs and deliver different results depending on those needs.

Interestingly, while the United States is considered the North Star in the constellation of democracy, population segments within the United States actually meet the broad criteria defined in Fox and Helweg's paper, commissioned by our government for nations considered less free. The definitions are provided below. As you read them, ask yourself which one applies to you, your issue of concern, or the community to which you or the issue are connected. The recommendations and information included in the following chapters are broad enough to support these three advocacy stages for individuals or groups. The important thing is for anyone interested in engaging as an enlightened citizen to know where he or she is in the process of advocacy.

Fox and Helweg advocacy definitions:

Transformational:
The ability of the marginalized or disadvantaged— the powerless or poor— to challenge the status quo by gaining a sense of their own power, includ-ing the capacity to define and prioritize their problems and then acting to address and resolve them.

Fox and Helweg also note this stage supports citizen empowerment and recognizes the fundamental tenet of democracy: that its overall health and strength ultimately derives from an enlightened and active citizenry.

Developmental:
The ability of citizens to organize themselves collectively to alter the exist-ing relations of power by providing themselves with a lasting institutional capacity to identify, articulate, and act on their concerns, interests, and aspirations, including the ability to achieve specific and well-defined policy outcomes.

This type of advocacy, the authors assert, carries with it, then, a commitment, value, or vision to balance the power between citizens and the government and the private (or market) sector. They add that a citizen organization or citizenry that is viewed to be and conducts itself as a legitimate partner in governance at the local and national levels is likely to be associated with a strong and healthy democracy.

> *Instrumental:*
> The process in which a group applies a set of skills and techniques to influence public decision making, ultimately achieving a well-defined social, economic, or political policy goal or reform.

According to Fox and Helweg, instrumental advocacy does not necessarily advance democracy; consider for example those special interest groups whose objectives may not support the public interest. For this reason, an informed and enlightened citizenry is needed to shape and influence the content of policies adopted by policymakers.

While these definitions describe separate advocacy stages, they often are interconnected elements of a dynamic process, with one often overlapping another. They can exist independently or simultaneously. They often involve fluid and strategically linked approaches that by no means are mutually exclusive.

The Three Ps

Different advocacy models require different approaches, but all of them enlist one or a combination of the three Ps. Getting what you want and need from the federal government requires that you do something: *participate*, *petition*, and if necessary, *protest*. The First Amendment gives each American the right to petition the government and to assemble peacefully. Participating and petitioning are less complicated than protesting. In fact, nonviolent protest often is enlisted as a last resort after all other strategies have failed and usually requires that groups comply with state and local ordinances to gather. Violent protest in America is a big no-no. For the purposes of this handbook, we will focus on the first two Ps: participation and petitioning. The chart that follows provides examples of permissible conduct related to each activity.

Power Point ⇨ More on the Three Ps

Twenty-two-year-old Molly Katchpole drew media attention when she used *petitions* available through Change.org that caused Bank of America and Verizon Wireless to reverse plans to increase customer fees. In terms of *protests*, the Occupy and Tea Party movements gained center stage using very different tactics in support of very different issues. From Cumberland University in Williamsburg, Kentucky (which is a source of relief for many families living in the hills of Appalachia), to the James Jordan Foundation (which is doing work in Africa and with the public schools of Chicago), everyday citizens are *participating* locally, nationally, and internationally to educate and provide clothing, food, shelter, health services, and more to persons living in diverse communities. Consider also the work of Dr. Michael DeBaun and Linda Anderson and their efforts to enlist the support of former Republican Senator Jim Talent and Congressman Danny Davis in the drafting, introduction, passage, and enactment of legislation that expanded services for persons who have sickle cell disease. The legislation was passed as an amendment to a jobs bill by a Republican-controlled Senate.

Activity	Permissible conduct
PETITION	Send letters, e-mails, phone calls; file law suits; draft legislation; and offer legislative proposals
PARTICIPATE	Engage in meetings, congressional and agency hearings, briefings, Capitol Hill Days, rule making, and public forums; conduct research; prepare educational materials; write grants; and bid on federal contracts
PROTEST/ PEACEFUL ASSEMBLY	Hold marches, vigils, and gatherings that typically require a permit and must be nonviolent to avoid arrest

Let's review what it takes to petition the government and participate in the process. In addition to making sure you have a congressional champion (where appropriate), you should know these basic facts:

- What you want to accomplish—your ideal result
- Who may have tried to do something similar
- When those others tried it
- How your idea differs from the one that was tried before
- Who your audience is
- Who has something to lose or win should your request be adopted
- Who you can count on in your neighborhood, community, county, or state to support your cause
- Who the other potential supporters are outside of your community, county or state
- Who will champion your cause at the national level
- How to develop and implement a plan of action
- How to make a specific request
- When to show up
- What to say in a meeting and who to take with you

Known as "federalism," our system recognizes four basic layers of governance—federal, state, county, and local. Understanding this framework is important because each layer has a distinct function and responsibility to citizens. For instance, a problem with trash pickup or a neighborhood school would be the concern of local government (mayor and city council or school board). Understanding who is responsible for what saves time and energy and helps avoid bureaucratic runarounds.

Layers of Government				
BRANCHES	FEDERAL	STATE	COUNTY	LOCAL
EXECUTIVE	president/ agencies	governor	county executive	mayor/city departments
LEGISLATIVE	Congress	state legislature/ general assembly	county commission	city council
JUDICIAL	Supreme Court and other federal courts	state courts	county courts	municipal, juvenile, family, and traffic courts

CHAPTER 8
Seven Basic Rules of Engagement

Effective advocacy involves several steps and requires a clear plan of action and strategy. Because advocacy is a way for citizens to pursue their passions, it is important to have fun and work on issues that mean the most to you! Also, the real secret to being effective is developing nurturing, positive, respectful relationships with neighbors, local leaders, other concerned stakeholders, beneficiaries, and elected officials during the processes of education, outreach, communication, and policy development.

Most advocacy approaches begin with policy articulation,—planning and strategy development,—and end with policy adoption and implementation. This chapter discusses seven basic areas of focus that apply to a comprehensive advocacy effort. Depending on where an organization or individual is in the process, these components can stand alone, be pursued in various combinations, or be aggregated as a collective plan of action. The seven areas are (1) policy articulation and development, (2) resource assessment, (3) community outreach (grassroots and grasstops), (4) policymaker outreach (secure champions and supporters, educate and influence others), (5) coalition building, (6) media and strategic communications, and (7) policy adoption and implementation.

The key to take away from the discussion that follows is that success at the national level doesn't just happen because your heart and head are in the right place on an issue. Once your heart and head are properly aligned and fired up on an issue, success requires strategic engagement.

Also, a well-defined strategy without doing something delivers nothing—not a thing. Similarly, a passionate plea for assistance or relief that has no strategy may kick up some dust, but ultimately it will die unfulfilled.

Step 1. Policy Articulation and Development: Know What You Want; Do Your Research

What issues or laws would you like to influence or change? What do you feel most strongly about? Those issues and concerns that affect us personally often have political relevance. Similarly, developments within the political realm have real-life, personal implications. The personal as political and the political as personal emerge as a real paradigm. The most successful advocacy occurs when folks are engaged with an issue of personal interest or relevance. The most effective governments are those most responsive to the will and interests of the people.

To begin, research your issue before taking any action! Investigate the Internet and other sources to see if others have expressed an interest in the same issue. Are others' concerns the same or similar to yours? Understand what action has or has not been taken. Also, check out any relevant congressional committee websites to see whether the issue is being addressed by Congress. In addition to accessing these sources, call the relevant staff person in the state or local office of your US senator or representative to determine the involvement of those offices. You sure would not want to ask your elected official to take action if action already is being taken. You may instead want to thank him or her for the assistance. This leads me to a final point: be prepared to take a position.

To be successful at the national level, enlightened citizen engagement means using advocacy approaches and techniques that reflect knowledge of rights, reclamation of power, and creation of new pathways of opportunity. Sounds complicated? Not really. The scenario when it plays out may be as simple as knowing that you have a right to request a meeting with an agency person, member of Congress, or congressional staff; claiming your power by writing and submitting a meeting request letter; and creating new pathways of opportunity by actually getting the meeting, accompanied by a commitment to act.

Advocacy at this level requires the articulation and development of an "ask," which is basically a specific request for what you want or need. In making a request, be sure you know how much the request will cost the federal government. Briefing materials have to be researched and prepared in a way that succinctly explains the key elements and objectives of the request. For initial meetings and communications, the average length of a briefing paper is one to three pages: short and simple. Additional in-depth information can always be shared as a supplemental communication to meetings, hearings, and briefings. For instance, if the goal is to ensure that inner-city youth eat healthy meals at school, be sure to do research on the issue, finding examples of how persons in the elected official's district or state are adversely affected and showing how the affected persons will benefit from the recommendation you propose.

Knowing which committees, agencies, accounts, and programs have jurisdiction over school lunch programs is critical. The school lunch programs fall under the jurisdiction of the Department of Agriculture, but it is important to note that the Department of Health and Human Services and the Office of the First Lady may also be sources of relevant information. As mentioned above, an Internet search will provide good leads, or you can contact one of the congressional offices representing the community where you live and request that the office obtains relevant information from the Congressional Research Service (CRS).

National associations or think tanks also may have relevant information and reports to share. If necessary, a think tank can be commissioned to undertake a report specific to a particular area of interest.

Power Point ⇨ Don't Be Shy

Hey, dude. It's their job! If there is an effort under way that is extraordinary—or conversely, causing harm—affecting you, your family, or others in your community, you need to inform federal policymakers. They are elected and paid to listen and serve. It is their job to assess and support (when appropriate) replication of exemplary efforts or to adopt prohibitions targeting programs and activities that may be causing harm or promoting inefficient use of federal resources.

One person's loss may be another's gain! Know from the outset that many folks may not agree with a particular position or that there may be at least one soul who may go out of the way to defeat an effort. No worries. Take an opportunity to understand the opposition and develop position statements that anticipate these concerns and compel leaders to support your recommendations. Address benefits, costs savings, and any other favorable attributes associated with your proposal. Benefits should outweigh any harm.

White papers or one pagers should be well written and visually attractive, including graphs and charts, current and comparative funding levels, and relevant data as appropriate. An outline template that is sometimes used includes the following sections: background, issue, recommended action, rationale or justification for the request, and next steps.

Step 2. Resource Assessment

In preparing to launch an outreach effort at the national level, and after articulating the desired results, it is important to assess the resources available or those that may be needed to support outreach, education, materials development, staffing, equipment, travel, office expenses, and lobbying at the national level. In particular, office resources—telephone, fax, computer, e-mail, and Internet access—are very important. A quality assessment should be translated into a budget, which may require a fund-raising approach to reach the desired implementation of the strategy. There's nothing quite like not having sufficient resources to complete what you start. If you have limited or no resources, move forward anyway, understanding what you will need as you enlist resources and supporters along the way.

Step 3. Community Outreach (Grassroots and Grasstops): Strength in Numbers

There is strength in numbers. Engaged constituent stakeholders or other constituent interests that share mutually relevant concerns or policy priorities often provide the relationship and knowledge equity to leverage access and impact. Elected and appointed officials understand what former House Speaker Tip O'Neil meant when he said, "All politics is local." There is nothing that grabs the attention of those seeking office like a mobilized, passionate, and knowledgeable group of constituents. Persons on the ground and affected by an issue are particularly relevant. These persons are often referred to as "grassroots." Another equally relevant category of players are those known as "grasstops," or people who are able to influence local, state, and national policy from strategically relevant leadership positions. They may be business, education, or faith leaders; city, county, or state officials; or nonprofit or association heads.

When engaging others, make sure you develop concise and well-written talking points and briefing materials to ensure everyone is on the same page. There are many venues for identifying and connecting with like-minded persons at the grassroots level: mosques, churches, synagogues, local coffee and gathering sites, labor unions, college campuses, neighborhood associations, professional and social associations, and social networking sites. Blogging also may extend your reach.

If you really want to go the extra mile, host an event for a small group of people who share your passion. Invite no more than fifteen people initially, and if you can get only two, that's a good start. The goal should be to develop concise talking points and a strategy to leverage the outreach and the numbers of folks and communications channels you engage. Again, make sure everyone uses the *same talking points*. Promoting separate agendas dilutes impact.

Step 4. Policymaker Outreach: Secure Champions and Supporters; Educate and Influence Others

If you are going to make waves in Washington, you must get someone to "carry your water." This phrase is an artful term often used in meetings on Capitol Hill. In meetings with staff persons, three questions typically arise: (1) what's your ask—what type of assistance are you trying to secure; (2) what member of Congress is championing your cause (carrying your water); and (3) how much does it cost? To be successful, an effort requires that there be at least one member of the House of Representatives and at least one member of the Senate who both support a specific ask and who are willing to push to carry it through enactment or completion of its course, whether the request involves legislation, appropriations, competitive grants, or regulatory relief. Ideally, champions should sit on committees and subcommittees of relevant jurisdiction or should hold an equally relevant position as a chair or ranking member, leader, or competitor in an important contested race for reelection. Inside Washington circles, it is well-known that members of Congress who are in contested races for reelection receive preferential treatment for their requests and issues they take a lead on as champions. The more senior the member, the better (more so if the member is in a contested race for reelection). Chairs and ranking members are particularly relevant. Selecting members of Congress who have a good working relationship with the president and the White House is also of significant value.

KEY POINTS:

Make sure you have a congressional champion: When it comes to making federal law, that authority rests in the hands of Congress. The president can propose legislation and must sign all legislation before it is enacted, but the writing and passage of legislation is the domain of the House and Senate. Therefore, if you seek legislation or a legislative modification, you must engage a member of Congress, or several, if you can. At a minimum, you need to have one who agrees to take the lead in getting a measure enacted. Ideally, that person will sit on a key committee or be a relatively senior player or otherwise be able to secure the ultimate adoption of the proposal. In a perfect world, you would have champions in the House and Senate. However, while having bicameral support is desired, it is not always required.

Know your audience: When meeting with members of Congress or the executive branch, do your research. Familiarize yourself with their congressional districts, where they grew up, their committee assignments and ranks, their political affiliations, and their policy priorities. Are they conservative, pro-choice, pro-war? Is there something in their personal story that may be relevant? Have they lost a child to violence or served in a war? Are they sensitive to rural, suburban, or urban issues? Are they fiscally conservative or socially liberal? Have they ever met you or do they share a mutual acquaintance with you?

Know when to show up: Be sure to get to Washington in time to make a difference. Congress, the White House, and federal agencies generally adhere to calendars of specifically scheduled events, including budget submissions, congressional hearings, legislative markups, floor action, and agency rule makings. To some extent, the congressional and agency calendars track the annual budget process and biennial election cycles. If you have an appropriations request, have it ready to submit no later than February of any given year. Make sure you complete required forms and remember that appropriations requests are good for only one year. If you seek authorization language, make sure you give yourself sufficient time to have a bill introduced or an amendment offered as part of related legislation being fast-tracked.

Make sure you assess the president's position on the issue: The president plays a key role in articulating vision and broad policy recommendations that affect every industry and community sector. Familiarize yourself with those positions, and make sure your ideas reflect an understanding of what has been proposed.

Step 5. Coalition Building

Coalitions are fundamental parts of any political process. The formation of groups that share common goals or interests is essential (most notably) to electoral politics, particularly presidential elections, where we see "soccer moms"; "swift-boat patriots"; and labor, LGBT, women's, and civil rights groups organizing and working together to support the same candidate or cause. Coalition dynamics are equally relevant at the local, county, and state levels. In Washington, outside of the campaign season, coalitions play an indispensable role in shaping, enacting, and implementing law and policy. Recall a key factor in the power equation: n(PEACE), the number of persons engaged and affected changes everything. Coalitions maximize reach and magnify impact.

Step 6. Media and Strategic Communications

Various media approaches can be used to educate, raise awareness, increase visibility, and enlist others to join a specific cause. With social media (including Facebook, YouTube, and Twitter), the ability to reach exponential numbers of folks, in real time, is profound. Uses of more traditional media and public relations strategies allow for a diversified approach and the direct targeting of policymakers where they move and live. For instance, writing letters to the editor; developing relationships with journalists at national and local news outlets; giving radio and TV interviews; advertising on billboards and signs generally but also on buses, and at malls, bus stops, and airports; petitioning; and organizing e-mail and postcard campaigns all have proven to be effective tools depending on the issue and available resources.

Step 7. Policy Adoption and Implementation (GOTV, Campaigns, and Elections as Necessary)

The whole point of enlightened citizen engagement is to finish what you start—to get those elected to office to do what they have been elected to do in a way that is codified as a matter of federal law, policy, or regulation. Furthermore, once a particular idea or request is approved as a matter of law, policy, or regulation, additional steps and outreach efforts are required to ensure that the initiative is funded and implemented properly to achieve the desired results in a way that is sustainable and scalable. With increased attention on accountability and performance-based metrics, the testing and evaluation of an effort may be the first step determining whether a project is sustainable or scalable and worthy of broad-scale adoption and robust funding.

If for some reason the idea or request has been enacted but not implemented or funded, the two-year (House of Representatives), four-year (president), and six-year (Senate) election cycles provide other avenues for engagement using get-out-the-vote (GOTV) and other campaign and election tools. Well-financed issue ads and campaign contributions by the superrich increasingly shape the election landscape. Middle-class, working-class, and poor people simply cannot afford to play that way. Even so, the antidote for those with fewer resources can be found through applying the power equation and making sure big money is countered with a big turnout of enlightened voters.

Power Point ⇨ Voting Is Only a First Step

Beyond turning out to vote, every American has a real opportunity to influence the composition of Congress by monitoring it and working to ensure that efforts at state, county, and local levels related to redistricting and voter registration are fair, support broad and equitable participation, and are not used to polarize communities based on ideology or otherwise undermine community cohesion.

A Basic Advocacy Model		
Action	**Requirements**	**Resources**
Policy Articulation & Development	• Know the issue • Research relevant material • Develop one pagers and briefing materials • Outline who, what, where, when, how and how much • Succinctly articulate the "ask"	• Vision and passion • Credible familiarity with the issue and understanding of the relevant federal process • Ability to help draft specific proposal language/ amendment (or engage someone who can)
Resource Assessment	• Identify how much funding and what type of resources are needed to support the advocacy effort • Host educational trips, briefings	• Budget • Funding streams and staffing resources • Persons to lead the government relations, public advocacy, lobbying or public education effort
Community Outreach (Grassroots & Grasstops)	• Convene a meeting of local stakeholders • Audit stakeholder strengths related to capacity and relationships • Adopt communication protocol • Identify and engage those leaders who have high-level relationships and connections from the business, civic and faith communities • Educate influential persons • Host targeted events • Develop synchronized messages • Engage allies	• Designation of appropriate staff resources for strategy development, coordination and follow-up • Concise and workable plan for engagement of grasstops
Educate & Influence Policymakers: Secure Champions	• Nurture, develop, and enlist the support of influential leaders in Congress who sit on relevant committees or have a relevant interest in your issue • Invite relevant leaders for site tours • Conduct meetings with members of Congress in their districts or states • Organize and engage stakeholders in Hill Days • Participate in town hall meetings • Present an award, develop a scorecard, or endorse those who support your cause • Participate, petition, protest	• Designate staff or point of contact • Leg work, phone work, boots on the ground • Appropriate resources to implement

A Basic Advocacy Model, cont'd		
Action	Requirements	Resources
Coalition Building	• Host targeted events • Build a coalition: identify persons and groups that have aligned interests • Develop synchronized messages • Engage allies	• Research relevant stakeholders • Relevant project leads or points of contact
Media & Strategic Communications	• Letters to the editor • Blogs • Talk radio, TV, social media, and Internet portals • Billboards, bumper stickers	• Engage PR or marketing consultant/expert • Designate capable spokesperson(s)
Policy Adoption & Implementation	• Ensure your proposal completes the process intact • Ensure your proposal receives funding or whatever resources are needed for implementation • Turn to electoral politics as complement to or alternative to outreach at the federal level	• Travel and office resources • Boots on the ground • Volunteer sweat equity • PAC or campaign fundraising support • Resources that maximize voter turnout • Issue ads/Super Pacs

Power Up: Plan of Action Checklist

Articulate intentions/vision/desired outcome:

_____

_____

_____

Communities and interests positively affected (by the proposal or the status quo)

- ❐ Particular industries or sectors (e.g., agriculture, banking, education, housing, child welfare, veterans)
- ❐ Certain populations (e.g., racial, ethnic, gender, disabled)
- ❐ Certain consumers
- ❐ Urban, rural, suburban communities

Communities and interests negatively affected (by the proposal or the status quo)

- ❐ Aligned interest groups and nonprofits
- ❐ Local or state leaders
- ❐ Business
- ❐ Academia
- ❐ Labor unions
- ❐ Religious
- ❐ Other

Targets

- ❐ Congress
- ❐ White House
- ❐ Federal agency
- ❐ Federal court
- ❐ Local (executive or legislative)
- ❐ State (executive or legislative)

Rationale

- ❐ Supported by research
- ❐ Supported by existing law
- ❐ Previously unidentified area of concern
- ❐ Community need
- ❐ Action needed to prevent harm
- ❐ Action needed to obtain federally relevant objectives

Congressional delegation

- ❐ US Senators
- ❐ US Representatives

Potential champions

❐ Federal	❐ Local
❐ State	❐ Faith
❐ Industry	❐ Other
❐ Celebrity	

Executive branch relevance (White House or federal agencies)

- ❐ Regional office (name) _____
- ❐ National office (name) _____
- ❐ White House—Office of Public Engagement
- ❐ White House—Faith-based institution
- ❐ Office of Management and Budget
- ❐ Office of the Secretary
- ❐ A particular agency or an office within a department or agency

Opposition

- ❐ Interest group
- ❐ Business/industry/other sector
- ❐ Nonprofit
- ❐ Religious
- ❐ Political

Preferred tools and tactics tied to the three Ps

- ❐ Write, call, e-mail DC and/or district
- ❐ Visit DC office
- ❐ Visit district office
- ❐ Petition online or use other mechanisms
- ❐ Nonviolent protest (in compliance with local or other relevant ordinances)
- ❐ Remove incumbent
- ❐ Retain incumbent
- ❐ Fill an open seat

Timeline

❐ Jan-March	❐ April-June
❐ July-Sept	❐ Oct-Dec

❐ Multiquarter

❐ Yearlong

❐ Multiyear

Available resources

❐ Financial

❐ Staff

❐ Volunteers

❐ Information technology

Resources required

❐ Financial

❐ Staff

❐ Volunteer

❐ Information technology

Media and communications

❐ Letter to the editor

❐ Newsletter

❐ Broadcast interviews

❐ Social media

❐ Marketing or PR pro

❐ Other

Election-related opportunities

❐ GOTV

❐ Town hall meetings

❐ Campaign contributions

❐ Voter registration

❐ Campaign volunteer

❐ Run for office

❐ Support or recruit a candidate

This form can be downloaded at www.anitaestell.com.

Completing the power up checklist is an important first step in developing a plan of action or strategy that specifically details intentions and what actions and resources are needed to realize the desired result. Once you've completed the checklist, action items can be plotted in the power grid. See the example that follows.

POWER GRID					
Power Equation	Vision x	Knowledge x	Power x	n (PEACE)	= Change
Power Line	Discover ➡	Develop ➡	Innovate ➡	Aggregate ➡	Sustain & Scale
Power Characteristics	Imagine & Visualize	Know the Issue	Plug In	Coalesce, Communicate, & Engage	Persevere & Lay a Foundation
Policy Articulation & Development	Identify what success looks like; visualize the end goal, and then develop plan that takes you from where you are to where you want to go Remove any blinders Let your heart be your compass and gauge and your brain your steering wheel	Using the Internet and other resources, research the issue Identify stakeholders and opponents Assess opportunities and obstacles Tap into your intangible strengths (awareness, intuition, and wisdom)	Plug into your passion and the energy source that fuels your FLOW Be open to creative approaches	Identify potential partners, other stakeholders, and those with a vested interest Assess potential reach and numbers of folks who can be engaged Enlist formal and informal tools to gauge interest and support for an issue—call a supporter and other allied folks, develop a questionnaire or conduct a poll, or access information developed by others	Assess how to maximize and sustain and scale impact, building upon a framework including performance metrics associated with inputs, outputs, benchmarks, and evaluative tools Be prepared to commit for the long haul
Resource Assessment	Assess what type of resources will be needed to get you from where you are to where you want to go Identify any expenses associated with staffing, transportation, research, media, marketing, or materials development	Assess whether there is a need to commission research by a think tank or other source	Stay plugged into the FLOW	Identify others who can make capital or in-kind contributions	Identify and secure human and fiscal resources needed to implement, sustain, and scale policy recommendations
Community Outreach: Grassroots & Grasstops	Identify persons, organizations, and leaders in the community you would like to have or who would be willing to support the effort	Identify how best to contact and engage them; secure referrals or personal introductions if needed Research the issues relevant or important to them Be clear about what you want them to do and how to engage	Stay plugged into the FLOW	Secure commitments that solidify a coalition Schedule regular meetings and appropriate communication chains Develop shared talking points	Secure commitments and participation up to and beyond implementation

Power Grid, cont'd					
Power Equation	Vision x	Knowledge x	Power x	n (PEACE)	= Change
Power Line	Discover ➡	Develop ➡	Innovate ➡	Aggregate ➡	Sustain & Scale
Power Characteristics	Imagine & Visualize	Know the Issue	Plug In	Coalesce, Communicate, & Engage	Persevere & Lay a Foundation
Educate & Influence Policymakers: Secure Champions	Identify the leaders in Congress or the executive branch you want to support your cause Be bold Identify those holding senior or key positions in leadership or on relevant committees	Do some research on the issues they care about, their personal stories, and their experiences that may connect with yours Provide sufficient information and research to expedite the adoption of policy	Believe	Assess whether coalition members, strategic partners, or supporters have any relevant connections or relationships Write letters and email Secure meetings in the district and in Washington, if appropriate Engage a consultant, if appropriate	Provide whatever assistance is needed and appropriate to obtain the desired results Revise the strategy as appropriate
Media & Strategic Communications	Think about who should know about the effort or your story	Consult or engage PR, cause marketer, communications person, or consultant	Keep an open mind Stay focused	Use social media to keep friends, partners, supporters, donors, and interested persons apprised	Publicize successes or any relevant challenges, from discovery to mass adoption
Policy Adoption & Implementation: GOTV, Campaigns, & Elections	Hold onto the vision	Work with relevant committees, subcommittees, and leadership teams to ensure final adoption If the effort fails, engage in election-related activities that may include GOTV, formation of an issue PAC, and fundraising as appropriate	Stay in the FLOW	Mobilize and engage as many like-minded folks as possible as you approach the finish line If the effort is derailed, take outreach, communications, and mobilization up a notch	Announce victory or roll up your sleeves and reengage as appropriate, reflecting on any lessons learned, strengths, weakness, and past scenarios

CHAPTER 9

Communicating with Elected Officials

A ny effective plan of action or advocacy effort must be supported by effective communications. The relevance of what is said, how it is said, when it is said, and to whom it is said cannot be overstated. Several avenues support direct communication with elected officials and their staff. The tone, timing, and tools should be assessed during the planning phase and throughout the process. It is important to document the responses and feedback received, as this information can be used to evolve the strategy, content, or approach to people and the process. This chapter addresses how to write to or meet with a federal official and how to request a meeting or request support for an issue. Sample letters and other materials are provided.

Write to the US Senate and the US House of Representatives: Depending on the issue, there may be times when you want to write only to federal policymakers. However, there also may be times when you want to enlist assistance from state and local leaders. If nothing else, you may be able to get local and state leaders to reach out in support of your efforts at the federal level. You may want to deliver your message by e-mail, hand or fax in addition to regular mail. Since the anthrax scare, mail delivery to congressional offices can take longer than it did prior to the scare. Before writing your representative, be sure to check out the sample letter provided in this chapter. Proper form is everything. Confirm receipt of your correspondence with a follow-up call. The competition for a member's attention is keen. See the graph that follows depicting more than a 500 percent increase in constituent mail between 2002 and 2010.

Meet with your elected officials in Washington and locally: Please remember, most members of Congress visit their congressional districts every week. If you are unable to come to Washington, request a meeting in your district with the legislator's scheduler. Be prepared to place this request in writing many days in advance. They often are home on Mondays and Fridays if there are no votes in DC. If you can get one or two other people who share your passion to join you, great. If the member is not available, then meet with the appropriate staffer. Depending on the issue, you may want to start with a meeting with a relevant staff contact. By having this meeting first, you can assess the member's position and sensitivities and share information with the staff contact, allowing the member to be briefed before meeting you. Participating in receptions, fund-raisers, faith-based and community events, town hall meetings, and other congressionally sponsored forums is another way to engage strategically. Remember: there's strength in numbers and consistently timely follow-up communications.

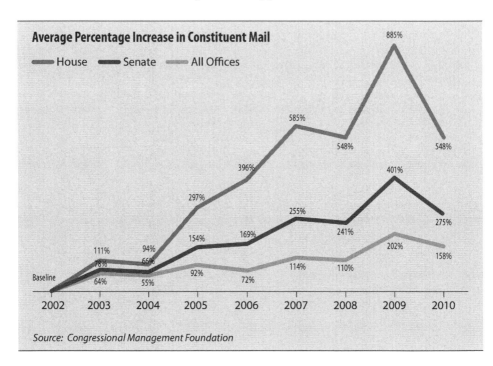

Source: Congressional Management Foundation

Research conducted by the Congressional Management Foundation confirms that when members have not yet made up their minds on an issue, in-person constituent meetings can be very important in persuading them. Of those members surveyed, 97 percent said in-person issue visits from constituents have some influence (51 percent) or a lot of influence (46 percent). Few said these visits had no influence.

Have a Capitol Hill Day: You can join a group with a presence in Washington or organize folks to participate in a day on Capitol Hill, visiting members of your congressional delegation and those who may sit on committees with jurisdiction over the issue that concerns you. Also consider:

- Contacting or appearing on talk radio

- Writing op-ed pieces for your local newspaper

- Writing a letter to the editor of local and national papers

- Posting your concerns on the Internet in a blog or on another site created by you or someone else

At some point, we all want resources and results. A successful advocacy effort will expand opportunities or fix a problem. Victory may take the form of a competitive grant, federal contract, legislative language, a resolution or executive order, participation in a hearing, submission of testimony, or service on a board or commission. Adherence to these approaches will drive the three outcomes you desire the most from Washington:

Congressional Influence Metrics		
	A Lot of Influence	Some Influence
In-Person Issue Visits from Constituents	46%	51%
Contact from a Constituent Who Represents Other Constituents	36%	60%
Individualized Postal Letters	20%	70%
Individualized E-Mail Messages	19%	69%
Phone Calls	14%	72%
Comments During a Telephone Town Hall	17%	68%
Visit from a Lobbyist	8%	74%
News Editorial Endorsement	10%	65%
Individualized Faxes	8%	62%
Form Postal Letters	1%	53%
Form E-Mail Messages	1%	50%
Postcards	1%	44%
Comments on Social Media Sites	1%	41%
Form Faxes	0%	30%
Source: Congressional Management Foundation		

access, action, and accountability. Treat a no as an invitation to negotiate, and keep going. Be sure to note any concerns about your request and modify your approach as appropriate. If your effort is not successful, next time, start earlier, make more noise, and engage more people.

The Value of Clear and Concise Writing: Sample Letter of Support to Send to Your Elected Official

Those elected to serve need to hear from you—whether you voted for them or not. They have a responsibility to represent all the constituents residing in their congressional districts. If you have any issues related to the federal government and what is happening in your community, after you vote, take your engagement to a whole new level by writing them to let them know your needs, interests, and concerns. After all, if you don't let them know, who will? There is a way to write a letter to ensure it is read and that congressional staff and representatives have sufficient information to take action. Ideally, a letter should be one page, and you should make your case in no more than two. Attachments may be included if necessary. Your letter should follow these guidelines:

- Let the member know up front that you live in his or her congressional district or state and are a constituent.
- Let the member know why you are writing in the opening paragraph.

- Be specific. Refer to specific legislation by name and bill number if you have it. Consult online sources, such as thomas.gov, to find this out.

- Keep it short, no longer than two pages.

- Avoid confrontational, accusatory, or inflammatory tones. A moderate tone substantiated by research, facts, or information on how the issue affects you personally is preferred.

- Include contact information for follow-up, and end with a courteous closing.

Other Action Items: Engage local champions, and ask them to contact members of Congress in support of your request. Potential supporters include:

- Local elected officials: mayor, city council members, county commissioners, and others

- Neighbors

- Religious leaders

- PTA or school leaders, university presidents

- Leaders of trade or professional associations, including labor unions

- Relevant nonprofits

- The business community

Sample letter for your member of Congress

The Honorable
US House of Representatives [US Senate]
Washington, DC 20515 [20510]

Dear Representative [Senator]_____:

As a constituent, I write now to ask for your immediate support in providing green-collar jobs. The stakes are high and the opportunities great. It is time for us to act to employ more Americans in jobs that reduce our greenhouse gas emissions and begin living more sustainably.

Specifically, I request your support in securing $500 million in funding in the Labor-HHS-Education appropriations bill for the Pathway Out of Poverty program. This program, funded by the US Department of Labor, will assist greatly in ensuring that unemployed, displaced, and low-income persons will be trained and able to secure green-collar employment, contributing to both the reduction of carbon emissions and the restored vitality of our nation's economy.

Your support of this program is important to me because I recently lost my job in the housing industry and hope to retool my skill set in a new area of national need. There are several green-jobs programs under way at the local level, but continuation of the effort will depend on whether federal funding is made available.

When you ran for election, you addressed energy challenges facing the nation and also indicated you would take proactive steps to fix our broken economy and bring jobs to those of us who live in your district. Support of the Pathway Out of Poverty program will contribute greatly to meeting those objectives.

I look forward to seeing action on these and related issues in the coming months, and I look forward to meeting with you in person to discuss these issues in greater detail.

Sincerely,

YesIcan

Oftentimes, sending a letter in support of an issue is not enough. A face-to-face meeting with the member may be required. A request for a meeting with a member of Congress should always be made in a letter (or at least an e-mail) that is shared with his or her scheduler or other appropriate staff person. A sample meeting request letter follows.

Sample meeting request letter

The Honorable [Name of Representative or Senator]
US House of Representatives [Senate]
Washington, DC 20015 [20010]

Dear Representative [Senator]_____:

On behalf of [name of organization], I write to request a meeting with you to discuss federal funding for [name project or program] and other [identify category (e.g., education, health, transportation)] issues of relevance to our organization and the nation. Specifically, I would like to discuss_____.

[Name of organization] is located in your congressional district [or state for senators]. Our mission is to_____.

The organization serves approximately _____persons annually.

In the spirit of our commitment to excellence, we want to enlist your input and assistance to ensure that local efforts and national priorities are in alignment. I welcome an opportunity to meet with you during the week of_____ or at another mutually convenient time.

I will be in touch with your scheduler to confirm your availability. Should you have any questions or concerns, please feel free to contact me directly. I may be reached at _____.

Thank you for considering this request.

Sincerely,

YesIcan

The Art of the "Ask": Got the Meeting; Get to the Point

So you have a meeting with a member of Congress. What should you do? What do you say?

The best issue in the world will go over like a lead balloon if you are not well prepared, take too long to explain, and basically don't understand the art of the "ask." You will hear this artful term often in reference to almost any issue or agenda: "What's the ask?" If you don't respond quickly and succinctly, you may be dismissed as a neophyte and invited to return after you figure out what you want.

If you do not have a specific request and seek an audience for another reason, that's fine also; just be sure to get to the point fast.

■ Elected officials are busy and typically distracted by competing demands for their attention. The biggest mistake people make when meeting with elected officials and policymakers is not knowing what they want, or if they do know it, hesitating or never making a hard ask. Big mistake. Elected officials and even federal employees are in those positions to serve, which is a privilege. That's why it is called public service. They are essentially servants of the people; so, it is their job to work for you. Always be able to summarize the issue and the nature of your request up front, in less than one minute. Do not waste much time with small talk. A little at the beginning of your meeting is fine. Try to make your presentation in about ten minutes. The meeting may take longer, but your summary of issues should be short, sweet and on point. You can always provide additional information in writing. When meeting at a reception or other public gathering, plan to have thirty seconds to one minute to make your point. Before approaching a public official in public, think about what to say and how you want to say it. If there is someone present who knows the person well, ask that person to introduce you.

For meetings in congressional offices

Know the issue:

■ Prepare briefing materials that are well researched and on point, graphically crisp, and grammatically concise. Be prepared to leave them behind, but make sure you keep a copy for yourself.

■ Know the briefing materials inside and out, and be prepared to answer questions about the briefing materials.

■ Ask questions if there are certain issues or aspects of the discussion you do not understand or need clarified.

■ Role-play in advance of the meeting.

■ Keep your message consistent and simple.

Know the member:

- Has he or she supported your organization in the past?
  If yes, be sure to thank the person with whom you are meeting for past and ongoing support.

- Focus on the priorities that have been identified in your materials, and target any items you know are of interest to the member.

- Describe how the issue and recommendations are relevant to the member's congressional district and constituency. Be sure you know the benefits and harm, the pros and cons, associated with your recommendation. Of course, you will raise only the positive points, but be prepared to address any concerns should they be brought up.

Managing group meetings:

- Have an agenda or short list of requests; everyone figuratively and literally should be on the same page.

- Designate a group spokesperson.

- Try to keep the group to a manageable number.

- One or two people are preferred, but definitely have no more than five. Depending on the issue, a larger group may be warranted, say, twenty folks. However, typical meetings in Washington with members of Congress in their personal offices have no more than four people in attendance, not including the members and their staff. Coalition and public-private partnership efforts, student groups, and advocacy days on Capitol Hill usually involve the presence of a larger group.

- Know what you want from the meeting, such as a commitment to a vote, a letter of support, or a discussion with committee chairpersons or ranking members on your behalf.

Listen up:

- Pay close attention to what the elected official and his or her staff have to say.

- Respond to any questions or concerns they may raise.
  If you do not know the answer, say so and promise to follow up with more detailed information.

Power Point ⇨ A Note About Protocol

What happens when you breach the protocol described here? It ain't pretty. Being disrespectful will get you escorted right out of a congressperson's office. Or consider the lobbyist who took his zeal for an issue too far: he cribbed a letter on congressional letterhead, which is illegal. He went to jail.

- When there are silent moments or long pauses in the discussion, be sure to ask questions that engage the staff or member.

- If you get someone who talks a lot but not about the issue you raise, be sure to return to the point you are trying to make.

Do's and don'ts during meetings:

- Do arrive on time.

- Do begin by thanking the legislator or staffer for past support of your organization (if appropriate) and for taking time to meet with you.

- Do state why you are concerned about the issue or issues. Your personal experiences are extremely valuable. Share examples, stories, and anecdotes to illustrate your points.

- Don't stay too long.

- Don't be disappointed if you are unable to meet directly with the policymaker. His or her assistant will be knowledgeable about the issue you will be discussing and will bring your points to the member's attention.

- Don't claim to be an expert. If you do not know an answer to a question, offer to find out and follow up at a later date. This will give you reason to communicate and express your views a second time.

- Don't be argumentative, although it is okay to disagree. Be polite but persistent as you make your points.

- Do end your meeting with two or three concise points about issues discussed.

- Do leave suggested letters and fact sheets on the issues you have addressed.

- Do build bridges that support a longer relationship.

Encourage the member to stay in contact, to engage you as an expert or as a resource. Make sure to bring up any relevant points that you may have in common with the member or identify persons you both may know.

- Do take notes. Follow-up is everything.

- Immediately after your meeting, jot down any questions raised and your impressions about the member's position on each issue discussed.

- If the legislator's view differed from yours, what was the basis for the disagreement? This information can be used for follow-up visits, letters, and phone calls.

- Don't give up, and be willing to revise your approach as needed.

Follow up your visit with a personal letter to the member. Express thanks for the opportunity to meet, and reiterate your main points. If staff members were present, write to them also. They can serve as important allies, resources, and advocates.

Visits to the nation's capital are most effective when they are planned in advance, which allows sufficient time to schedule meetings, reserve hotels, arrange transportation, prepare briefing materials, schedule speakers, and secure resources to pay for the trip.

The forms and worksheets that appear on the next few pages may be downloaded at www.anitaestell.com.

Trip Planning Worksheets

Number of travel days _____ Number of days in Washington _____

How much money do you or does your organization have available for travel and expenses?_____

Do you need to raise additional funds?_____

How will you secure the funds for the trip? _____

_____

Who will take the lead in securing resources or organizing fundraising efforts? _____

_____

Will each individual be responsible for his or her expenses? _____

_____

Is there sufficient time to negotiate reduced group rates for travel and hotel? _____

_____

Who will lead the logistics planning for the trip?_____

_____

Who will facilitate follow-up communications and confirmations with hotels, Hill offices, attendees, transportation providers, and others? _____

_____

Do any rooms or catering arrangements need to be reserved?_____

_____

Will there be a need for floor passes, White House tickets, or tours? _____

_____

Organization	Address	Telephone
Hotel Information		
Charter Bus Information		
Airline Information		
Consultant Information		
Speaker Information		
Tickets or Tours		

The following worksheet itemizes anticipated expenses for any trip to Washington.

Budget	
Expense Item	Amount
Airfare	
Ground Transportation	
Other Transportation	
Lodging	
Daily Food (Breakfast)	
Daily Food (Dinner)	
Miscellaneous Food	
Presentation Materials	
Entertainment	
Miscellaneous	
Emergency Cash	
Grand Total	

Go to www.anitaestellblog.com or the official House and Senate sites for a complete list of members of Congress. The House site is www.house.gov and the Senate site is www. senate.gov. Click on the appropriate menus to find the directories.

The following worksheet allows those planning to meet with members of Congress to track and record their communications for future reference and follow-up. Beyond recording this information, it is very important to build rapport and positive relationships with persons listed on this sheet.

Congressional Office Contact Sheet	
Name of Lawmaker	
Name of Scheduler	
Chief of Staff	
Office Contact E-Mail Address	
Office Telephone	
Political Affiliation	
Contact Log	
Date of Contact	Notes
Date of Contact	Notes
Date of Contact	Notes
Date of Contact	Notes
Date of Contact	Notes
Date of Contact	Notes

Reproduce as many copies of this table as needed. You also may download it at www.anitaestell.com.

Document and list all persons attending the meeting or making the trip to Washington. You may also wish to create a communications stream through email, Google, LinkedIn, Facebook, or another social network group.

Before going to a meeting with an elected official or his or her staff, role-play with other group members and test yourself on your familiarity with the meeting process and the issues you plan to raise.

Attendees		
Name	E-mail	Telephone
Note: Extend or reproduce this sheet as needed.		

Test yourself! Are you ready to answer key questions?

Can you clearly and succinctly articulate, verbally and in writing, what action you would like taken on Capitol Hill, at an agency, or within your state or community? Please write it in one or two sentences here.

What key individuals or lawmakers would you like to meet with during your trip?

Is your issue currently under consideration or will it be under consideration at the national level?

What is the issue's status in terms of committee or floor action?

Who are the issue's proponents or sponsors? Who are the opponents in Congress or within the executive branch?

Who in your group will be the key point of contact for your state's lawmakers?

How many people belong to or are represented by your organization?

How many people support your request? Who are they? Is there another organization or group that shares this same interest? There is power in numbers, and they show elected officials that this issue has broad appeal and is not a self-issue.

How many persons are affected by your request? Is the issue already advocated by an established organization? If so, be sure to take a look at what that organization is doing on Capitol Hill to become better informed before contacting lawmakers.

What is your representative's or senator's voting history on the issue?

Resources for Contacting Members of Congress and Congressional Leaders

In an age of increased transparency, accountability, access to information, and public participation, there are multiple ways to let Congress know what is on your mind. Both the House of Representatives and the Senate have operator assistance and websites to help you directly reach members and their staff.

US House of Representatives

By mail:
The Honorable [Name]
US House of Representatives
Washington, DC 20515

By phone:
(202) 225-3121

Online:
All members and committees: house.gov
Office of the Speaker: speaker.house.gov
Office of the Democratic Leader: democraticleader.house.gov
Office of the Democratic Whip: democraticwhip.house.gov
Office of the Republican Leader: republicanleader.house.gov

US Senate

By mail:
The Honorable [Name] US Senate
Washington, DC 20510

By phone:
(202) 224-3121

Online:
All senators and committees: senate.gov
Democratic leadership: democrats.senate.gov
Republican leadership: republican.senate.gov

Contact federal, state and local leaders:

Two of my favorite sources, congress.org and votesmart.org, include information on federal, state, and local officials. Type in the constituent ZIP code when you get to each site.

Monitor congressional activity:

Several resources keep citizens apprised of what is happening in Washington. Notices of most events, briefings, floor proceedings, hearings, press conferences, and other events are published in advance. Many proceedings are broadcast on the web and on other media in real time. See the following sources for schedules and access to live coverage of hearings and other proceedings.

Watch hearings:
>   c-span.org
>   capitolhearings.org
>   openhearings.org
>   ustream.tv (for House of Representatives)

Obtain hearing testimony:

Access the appropriate committee website through house.gov or senate.gov, or call the relevant committee using the Capitol switchboard, (202) 225-3121.

For a record of floor proceedings:

See the *Congressional Record*, the official record of House and Senate floor proceedings, at gpoaccess.gov, and view thomas.gov.

Subscription services:

Congressional Quarterly (cq.com); *Gallerywatch* (gallerywatch.com); *National Journal* (nationaljournal.com)

Official oversight and reports:

The *US Government Accountability Office (GAO)*, gao.gov, is an independent, nonpartisan agency that works for Congress. Often called the "congressional watchdog," GAO investigates how the federal government spends taxpayer dollars. The head of GAO, the comptroller general of the United States, is appointed to a fifteen-year term by the president from a slate of candidates proposed by Congress.

The *US Government Printing Office (GPO)*, gpo.gov, disseminates official information for all three branches of government. It's also a great resource for tracking legislation.

Upon the request from a member of Congress, the *Congressional Research Service (CRS)*, a division of the Library of Congress, will research a particular issue or set of issues. Some of its reports are available online at the CRS website, see also opencrs.org.

Track legislation:

It may take years for a bill to pass. Often, when a bill is not passed before a new session of Congress commences (every four years), it may be reintroduced with a different name or new bill number. Tracking a bill online can help you monitor deliberations associated with a measure. Check the following sites:

>   thomas.gov
>   congress.org (a fee may be required)
>   govtrack.us
>   gpoaccess.gov
>   washingtonwatch.org

Capitol Hill print media:

Numerous publications provide detailed coverage of Congress, the White House, and federal agencies. Inside the Beltway, the most popular daily and weekly sources of information are:

Congressional Quarterly, cq.com
National Journal, nationaljournal.com
Politico, politico.com
Roll Call, rollcall.com
The Hill, thehill.com

Petitions:

Change.org is the world's largest online petition platform directed toward empowering communities seeking change.

www.350.org represents a global movement organized to solve the climate crisis and provides a solid example of grassroots mobilization, online campaigns, and mass action.

http://petitions.whitehouse.gov is the official site to start or sign a petition for consideration by the president and White House.

www.ipetitions.com has collected more than 17 million signatures and supports online activism and democratic engagement.

Resources for contacting the president, the first lady, and the executive branch

White House:

Established in 1939, the Executive Office of the President (EOP) consists of a group of federal agencies serving immediately under the president. Among the oldest of these are the White House Office, where many of the president's personal assistants are located, and the Office of Management and Budget. Public interaction with the White House occurs via e-mail, regular mail, requested meetings, invitations, town hall meetings, select speaking engagements, other public forums, and White House tours. Official public outreach and related activities are managed by the Office of Intergovernmental Affairs and Public Engagement. The White House website, whitehouse.gov, is the best way to monitor the president's priorities and public activities.

On matters related to public policy, emails and text messages should never be used as a substitute for the development of working relationships with key staff and the proper submission of well-drafted policy recommendations to these persons. To develop these relationships or if you would like to meet one-on-one with White House staff on policy issues, the best place to start is the Office of Intergovernmental Affairs and Public Engagement, unless, of course, you have contacts or friends in high places. Or, you may call or write to the president:

The White House
1600 Pennsylvania Avenue NW
Washington, DC 20500

(Please include your e-mail address)

Should you need a response because a matter is time sensitive or for another reason, please reach out by phone. You can find direct contact information through a selection of leadership directories available for purchase. Finally, if appropriate, enlist help from someone who represents you in Congress.

White House Contact Information:
Comments: 202-456-1111
Switchboard: 202-456-1414
Visitors Office: 202-456-2121
Fax: 202-456-2461

Office of the Vice President: vice_president@whitehouse.gov

Office of the First Lady, Michelle Obama:
The White House
1600 Pennsylvania Avenue NW
Washington, DC 20500
http://www.whitehouse.gov/administration/first-lady-michelle-obama

Office of Management and Budget (OMB), http://www.whitehouse.gov/omb/: The core mission of OMB is to serve the president of the United States in implementing his/her vision across the executive branch through budget development and execution. OMB is the largest component of the Executive Office of the President.

Office of Public Engagement (OPE), http://www.whitehouse.gov/administration/eop/ope: As part of making the government accessible to its citizens, the OPE coordinates public speaking engagements for the administration and the various departments of the Executive Offices of the President. OPE works to improve public awareness and involvement in the work of the administration.

Office of Intergovernmental Affairs (IGA), http://www.whitehouse.gov/administration/eop/iga: The IGA works closely with state, tribal, and local officials elected by the American people to ensure America's citizens and their elected officials have a government that works effectively for them and with them. State, tribal, and local governments are critical to the creation and implementation of national policy.

The **National Economic Council (NEC),** http://www.whitehouse.gov/administration/eop/nec, advises the president on US and global economic policy. It resides within the Office of Policy Development and is part of the Executive Office of the President. By executive order, the NEC has four principal functions: to coordinate policymaking for domestic and international economic issues, to coordinate economic policy advice for the president, to ensure that policy decisions and programs are consistent with the president's economic goals, and to monitor the implementation of the president's economic policy agenda.

The **Domestic Policy Council (DPC),** http://www.whitehouse.gov/administration/eop/dpc/, coordinates the domestic policymaking process in the White House and offers advice to the president. The DPC also supervises the execution of domestic policy and presents the president's priorities to Congress.

Federal agencies and commissions: There are hundreds of federal agencies and commissions charged with handling such responsibilities as managing America's space program, protecting its forests, and gathering intelligence. For a full listing of federal agencies, departments, and commissions, visit http://www.usa.gov/Agencies/Federal/All_Agencies/index.shtml

CHAPTER 10

Lessons Learned: The Awakening

This book is intended to be about truth—that truth that nurtures life, fosters peace and prosperity, and enlightens the human experience in such a way that manifests positive and constructive results within neighborhoods, communities, and the nation. Once we achieve these objectives as human beings, we will have done something truly magnificent.

Speaking about truth is like talking about trash and treasure. It has been said that one person's trash is another person's treasure. In politics and law, one person's truth often is another person's lie. But we also know that there are certain truths that are self-evident, including the one that says all persons are created equal and endowed by the Creator with certain inalienable rights, which include life, liberty, and the pursuit of happiness.

Within the personal, political, and government realms, our fondest aspirations are the same: to be better and do better. In the United States, realization of these ideals requires that we hold government accountable, and to do that, we, the people, must engage. Engagement requires vision, commitment, passion, courage, and an awareness of the potential, power, and promise of being human. It requires "us" to align our thoughts, words, and deeds with the best we have to offer, what Gary Zukov called the "highest parts of ourselves."

Three types of citizens are profiled in the first part of the handbook: the law abiding, advocates, and revolutionary. Enlightened citizenship and collective action require more than just obeying the law. Franklin D. Roosevelt reminded us that we must engage our thinking and good works around efforts that reflect a unity of purpose.

What I have learned (and attempt to share) is that good citizenship is inextricably linked to our status as human beings, which involves the interplay of the dynamic and seemingly dualistic influences of the physical and spiritual, material and nonmaterial, conscious and unconscious, esoteric and exoteric, and both art and science. To the naked eye within the political and socioeconomic realms, some of these influencing forces look like Republican versus Democrat, rich versus poor, black versus white, management versus labor, urban versus rural, young versus old, war versus peace. To the intuitive and attuned, dichotomization of issues and communities just doesn't feel right in the gut. We know in our heart of hearts that such discourse is neither healthy nor helpful.

The challenges and opportunities we face as we engage will be defined by the roles we assume as citizens and will reflect the essence of who we are at our collective core—and how we see and treat each other. As Paul Rogot Loeb observes in *Soul of a Citizen*, "Overcoming our instinctive withdrawal requires courage. It requires learning the skills and developing the confidence to participate. . . . It also requires creating a renewed definition of ourselves as citizens."

A former governor of my home state of Illinois, Adlai Stevenson, in his book, *Wit and Wisdom*, once said, you and I "as citizens of this democracy, are the rulers and the ruled, the lawgivers and the law-abiding, the beginning and the end." Ultimately, in our system, the challenge and the blessing have everything to do with how effectively we balance and protect the coexistence of these roles, with the understanding that all people are of equal value.

Even so, we know there is no inevitability to freedom, justice, or progress. Achievement of these objectives requires commitment, vision, and sacrifice. We know that ignorance is dangerous, complacency is passé, and apathy comes with a price too high to pay. Thankfully, the archives of knowledge and ancient wisdom are now widely accessible through contemporary communications systems. What we don't know, we can learn. What we don't have, we can create. The American system works best when the people dare to believe and do, when they are conscious and informed, and when they are motivated by compassion and constructively engaged. There are so many examples of how "regular" folks have influenced the process and substance of making law, from the Amber Alert system and the Lilly Ledbetter Fair Pay Act to Rosa Parks and Elizabeth Glaser's advocacy on behalf of pediatric AIDS reform.

Our success as a national community of interests has depended and will continue to depend on how Americans pursue higher ideals and strategies that help and heal. As the Reverend Martin Luther King Jr. once said, "Our hope for creative living in this world house that we have inherited lies in our ability to re-establish the moral ends of our lives in personal character and social justice. Without this spiritual and moral reawakening, we shall destroy ourselves in the misuse of our own instruments."

If you could change one thing at the national level, what would it be? Think about it. Tomorrow will be shaped by policies adopted by the government now. The operative word is *now*. Pick an issue. There already are so many on the agenda—federal spending, banking, climate change, education, energy use and conservation, health care, jobs, returning veterans, Medicare, Medicaid, national security, and Social Security. Rather than discussing these issues in detail, my goal has been to expand your understanding and spark your curiosity in the federal government and how it works. I have outlined the fundamental principles upon which we can take a stand. I have shared stories, power equations, and other tools for those who want to act like citizens but think like revolutionaries.

Let us move forward boldly, knowing that the future and good fortune favor the prepared and engaged and understanding that America's fate depends on how well we sideline our differences. This responsibility rests not only with elected officials; it primarily falls on those who rule—the people. The real power is not inside Washington: it resides within each of us and within our communities.

Going forward, remember the basic formula: Vision x Knowledge x Power (FLOW) x n(PEACE) = Change. If it were a word equation, it would read as follows: May your vision guide you; wisdom ground you; faith, love, opportunity, and will strengthen you; and magnitudes of others join you in the realization of meaningful achievements that benefit family, community, the planet, and humankind.

SECTION THREE

Appendices

APPENDIX A

The American Story is Our Story

We hold these truths to be self-evident, that all men [and women] are created equal, that they are endowed by their Creator with certain unalienable Rights, that among these are Life, Liberty and the pursuit of Happiness.—That to secure these rights, Governments are instituted among [Persons], deriving their just powers from the consent of the governed,—That whenever any Form of Government becomes destructive of these ends, it is the Right of the People to alter or to abolish it, and to institute new Government, laying its foundation on such principles and organizing its powers in such form, as to them shall seem most likely to effect their Safety and Happiness.—The Declaration of Independence, July 4, 1776

Today, we find ourselves again reaching to rise. This time, new demographic communities will constitute the majority and will be needed to rebuild, sustain a prolonged recovery, and reposition America in the global community. With the growth of minority populations and the growing influence of women, America quickly is becoming a majority-minority and female-influenced nation.

This Land is Your Land—Mine, Too

It's not revisionist history to insist that the American story belongs to all of us. Sure, the Great Man Theory survives, but many people great and small, male and female, have contributed significantly to what has become the world's most successful exercise in democracy. Consider the following people:

Bernardo de Galvez (1746-1786): Kept the British from coming

America wouldn't be what it is today without Bernardo de Galvez, the Spanish military leader who had the back of the original thirteen colonies. De Galvez defeated the British in Florida during the Revolutionary War, keeping the empire from getting a foothold in the South. Many places are named for him, notably Galveston, Texas.

Nanye-hi (1738-1822): Beloved and brave

Nanye-hi, also known as Nancy Ward, was a Cherokee leader who took colonist Bryant Ward as her second husband. Nanye-hi worked to keep peace between her people and white settlers by promoting coexistence over war. Dubbed "Beloved

Woman," Nanye-hi put her principles on the line many times when she sided with settlers to avoid violence.

Deborah Sampson Gannett (1760-1827): Fought for the American ideal

Deborah Samson Gannett fought in the Continental Army during the Revolutionary War by impersonating a man. Calling herself Robert Shurtleff, she was wounded in combat and honorably discharged.

James Armistead Lafayette (1760-1830): Slave, spy, and patriot

James Armistead Lafayette, considered one of the most important Revolutionary War spies, was in fact a double agent. Because he posed as a runaway slave, the British thought he had been hired to spy on the Americans. Instead, he had been placed in the British camp to spy on General Charles Cornwallis. Armistead eventually would be credited with supplying the information that helped to win the battle at Yorktown, which crippled the British military and resulted in their surrender on October 19, 1781.

Going forward, *all* Americans must know of their important connection to a unique story. They must know the difference between *fighting for* and *having* rights. This issue came up during a radio show I was hosting. I had paired former Representative Ronald V. Dellums with a much younger political activist in Detroit, Ajene Evans. During that conversation, Evans expressed frustration that the younger generation still needed to fight for their rights. "What do you mean, fight for your rights?" Dellums asked. "We did that. You don't have to fight for your rights. You have rights!" Then there was silence, for just a moment. The young brother—*snap!*—got it. What Dellums said made a world of sense. You don't have to fight for what is already yours. Take a moment. Think about it. What is your story and your family's story in relationship to the American experience? Are you an owner of the story, a contributor, beneficiary, victim, or observer, or are you just numb, doing enough to get by? Whatever the case, your status as a human being comes with numerous rights and privileges.

An Architecture of Belief

The Declaration of Independence, severing all allegiance to the British Crown in 1776, the Bill of Rights and the US Constitution remind us of who we are. Like the string threaded through kernels of popcorn, the basic tenets of these documents connect Americans and provide a set of ideals that empower people more than government. We are citizens, not subjects. We have proven ourselves most revolutionary when faced with tyranny and fired up in a fight for freedom. Peter De Bolla, in *The Fourth of July and the Founding of America*, in telling the American story, notes that something fundamental and very significant occurs in the declaration of a new kind of belief structure:

> The story of the Fourth of July presents a supreme fiction that the nation
> came into being on a particular day in 1776. It does not matter in terms of
> the coherence of the story whether or not this has any basis in fact. It does

not matter insofar as one subscribes to this story that nations, complex geopolitical organisms, are never founded at a single stroke. For in telling this story something fundamental and very significant occurs: the declaration of a new kind of belief structure. We have it in our power to determine what shall be taken to be a self-evident truth. . . . And in that collectively imagined common tongue "America" by simple force of a declaration is founded. In celebrating independence . . . may it also be remembered that . . . the declaratory act that founds America, created and continues to create an architecture of belief, which, for both good and ill, has power to change the world.

The observations of De Bolla, who, by the way, was a King's College fellow at Cambridge University when he wrote the above passage, remind me of King George III. You may recall that King George ruled Great Britain when a renegade colony known as America had the gumption to declare war against Britain. The movie *The Madness of King George* chronicles the king's bouts with a nervous/mental ailment. He ruled for sixty years, from 1760 to 1820, after taking the throne at age twenty. In one scene in the movie, a visibly agitated George says, "Peace of mind! I have no peace of mind. I have had no peace of mind since we lost America. Forests, old as the world itself, plains, strange delicate flowers, immense solitudes. And all nature new to art. All ours. Mine. Gone. A paradise lost!"

This dusty piece of real estate we call home, and sometimes take for granted, actually represents, no, embodies something much more: "an architecture of belief, which, for both good and ill, has the power to change the world," and for those who would be tyrants or kings, "a paradise lost." We are a people who hold certain truths to be self-evident: each of us, no matter our race, religion, gender, and sexual orientation, is endowed with certain inalienable rights, including life, liberty, and the pursuit of happiness. There is no properly sanctioned government without the consent of the governed. Moreover, when the government becomes "destructive of these ends," then "it is the right of the people to alter or abolish it."

Americans have learned (albeit the hard way) that greed, meanness, and ignorance make a toxic cocktail, particularly deadly when mixed with fear and stirred with lies. We have developed a muscularity associated with certain core, constitutionally based principles written on paper and given life by the people. Some have compared the American experience to a melting pot or salad bowl. I think of it as a combination—a stew, a fluid, textured merging of a distinct composition of seasonings, flavors, and ingredients that takes on new properties when simmered and stirred in a common pot. This experience is supported by key foundational principles that provide the framework for the efficient operation of our government today.

APPENDIX B

A Quick Note About Your Bill of Rights

Beyond the Declaration of Independence, the document that grounds our form of democracy and connects us across space, time, and family origin is the Bill of Rights. Written by James Madison, the Bill of Rights contains ten provisions added as amendments to the US Constitution. The Constitution was drafted in 1787 and became effective in 1789. The Bill of Rights was approved in 1791.

The Bill of Rights was added after the Constitution was fully ratified because of concerns about a tendency to overemphasize government management over the rights of people. Therefore, when reviewing the Constitution, you will notice two themes: (1) protection of individual rights, and (2) the organizational architecture of the American form of government. The first eight amendments enumerate the rights of the people. The Ninth and Tenth Amendments describe the relationship between the people, the state governments, and the federal government. Collectively, these amendments guarantee certain freedoms and rights and thus are known as the Bill of Rights.

Some of the first ten amendments are well known, particularly the First Amendment, which protects freedom of speech, religion, and association. All ten amendments, and the freedoms they guarantee, are:

Amendment 1: Freedom of religion, press, expression

Amendment 2: Right to bear arms

Amendment 3: Protection from the quartering of soldiers

Amendment 4: Protection against search and seizure

Amendment 5: Rights in trial and punishment, compensation for eminent domain takings

Amendment 6: Right to speedy trial by jury, right of accused people to be confronted by witnesses against them

Amendment 7: Right to trial by jury in civil cases

Amendment 8: Protection against cruel and unusual punishment

Amendment 9: Right to additional protections not otherwise listed in the Constitution

Amendment 10: States' rights

APPENDIX C
Three Branches of the Same Tree

The federal government as established by the Constitution consists of three branches of government and is organized around the principle of constitutional checks and balances. Each branch—the legislative, executive, and judicial—has some authority to act on its own and some authority to influence the other two branches. Each branch, in turn, also is influenced by the other branches. Despite their distinct roles, these are three branches of the same tree, with roots planted in the same source and limbs that share a common destiny.

Power Point ⇨ Getting Your Money's Worth

The roles of the legislative, executive, and judicial branches of the federal government are not self-sustaining. Their smooth operation requires significant resources and other types of checks that have to be balanced. I'm talking about good ol' fashioned money provided by taxpayers. But for revenues generated from tax payments, fees, and borrowing from other countries, a good number of folks who work for the federal government might have to find employment elsewhere. The operation of America is literally classified as an industry. Recall the implications associated with the government shutdown of 2013.

Consider also: The Bureau of Labor Statistics, on its website www.bls.gov, identifies the federal government as a significant source of employment. It notes:

- The federal government is the nation's largest employer;

- The federal government employs approximately two million people;

- Most, 85 percent, of the federal workforce works outside of Washington, DC; and

- Significant job openings will emerge with a growing number of federal employees retiring over the next several years.

Employment Breakout by Branch

The legislative branch employs about only 1 percent of federal workers, the majority of whom work in the Washington, DC, area.[1]

---

[1] Article I, Section I of the US Constitution vests all legislative powers in the United States Congress, which consists of the Senate and House of Representatives.

Of the three branches, the executive branch[2] is the largest and most programmatically diverse. It employs about 97 percent of all federal civilian employees (excluding Postal Service workers).

The judicial branch[3] employs about 2 percent of federal workers, and unlike the legislative branch, its offices and employees can be found across the country.

Even with all of the checking and balancing, accompanied by heated rhetoric and sometimes tense posturing, this model has worked. Maybe it's because deep down we recognize the principle shared by America's original inhabitants—the Native Americans—one of whom said, "The branches of a tree should never be so foolish as to fight amongst themselves."

The Legislative Branch

The structure of the House and Senate is designed to ensure the equitable representation of (1) smaller but densely populated states and (2) larger but sparsely populated states.

The Senate has 100 members, with each state having two elected members, regardless of size or population. The House of Representatives has 435 members, with each state's representation dependent upon its population. Each House member represents a specific geographic district within the state, while senators represent their whole state. In total, the 535 members of Congress represent more than 300 million people. Both the House and Senate have specific duties:

The House	The Senate
Must be the source of any budget bills	Can confirm or reject any treaties the president establishes with other nations
Can initiate laws, including taxing and spending measures	Responsible for confirming presidential appointments of cabinet members, federal judges, and foreign ambassadors
Can decide whether public officials should be tried if accused of a crime	Tries any federal official accused of a crime after the House votes to impeach that official
Representatives are elected to two-year terms, every two years.	Senators are elected to six-year terms, in staggered election cycles. The vice president presides over the Senate and has the right to cast a vote in the event of a tie.

---

2 Article II, Section I of the US Constitution vests (chief) executive power in the president of the United States, who shall hold office for a term of four years, together with the vice president.

3 Article III, Section I of the US Constitution vests the judicial power of the United States in one Supreme Court and several lower courts with original and appellate jurisdiction over federal issues.

While the duties and powers of the House and Senate differ, collectively Congress is responsible for passing laws that hold our nation together and that define our international relationships and activities. Congress also has the power to declare war. These powers are strictly given to the legislative branch by the Constitution. In addition to creating laws, one of Congress's most important activities is appropriating funding that makes the executive branch operational and providing executive branch oversight. Congress may hold hearings to investigate the operations and actions of the executive branch to ensure it is carrying out the law with integrity.

The Executive Branch

This branch of the US government has two primary areas of authority and responsibility—domestic policy and foreign affairs. Within the realm of domestic policy, the president has the authority to oversee the execution and implementation of the law. Through the ability to veto laws proposed by Congress, shape the federal budget, promulgate regulations and agency guidance, and appoint key federal positions, the president has the ability to significantly influence the legislative and judicial branches.

Additionally, the president can make sweeping changes that affect domestic policy through the issuance of executive orders (EO). Unlike laws, which require months to pass and the consent of Congress, EOs allow presidents to use their executive authority to order federal agencies to implement new policies.

In addition to shaping domestic policy, the direction of our nation's defense and security efforts is led by the executive branch. The Constitution establishes the president of the United States as the commander-in-chief of the armed forces.

The president serves as the head of the executive branch. Under the president's leadership are a cabinet, including the vice president and the heads of fifteen executive departments: the secretaries of agriculture, commerce, defense, education, energy, health and human services, homeland security, housing and urban development, interior, labor, state, transportation, treasury, and veterans affairs, and the attorney general (head of the Department of Justice). The tradition of the cabinet dates back to the beginnings of the presidency itself. Most issues affecting Americans fall under the jurisdiction of these fifteen major departments, which take the lead in managing programs and distributing funding approved by Congress.

Power Point ⇨ Separate But Complementary Powers

Congress makes laws and federal agencies enforce those laws. Congress legislates and federal agencies regulate. For instance, Congress created and funds programs under the Clean Air Act. The Environmental Protection Agency (EPA) enforces this law through regulations related to emissions and air quality standards.

The Judicial Branch

The federal courts of the United States make up this branch, which considers legal cases that challenge or require interpretation of legislation passed by Congress and signed by the president. It consists of the Supreme Court and the lower federal courts. Appointees to the federal bench serve for life or until they voluntarily resign, retire or are impeached.

The Supreme Court is the most visible of all the federal courts. It is the nation's definitive judicial body, and it makes the highest rulings. The number of justices is determined by Congress rather than the Constitution. Since 1869, the court has been composed of one chief justice and eight associate justices. Justices are nominated by the president and confirmed by the Senate.

Like the other branches of government at the federal level, the judicial branch has checks and balances placed upon it. As referenced previously, the president appoints the members of the court, and the Senate confirms them and has the power to impeach them. In certain circumstances, the Supreme Court can declare laws of Congress and acts of the president unconstitutional.

US Supreme Court decisions usually follow the appeal of a decision made by one of the regional courts of appeals (which consider cases appealed from the district courts and the Court of Appeals for the Federal Circuit) or a state supreme court. There is at least one district court located in each state, but most states have multiple courts and multiple judicial districts. The state of Texas, for example, has four judicial districts—northern, western, southern, and eastern. Each judicial district has multiple courts (judges sitting in different cities), which are typically the first courts to hear most cases under federal jurisdiction.

APPENDIX D

The People's Money: The Federal Budget and Why It Is a Big Deal

Many years ago, the late Benjamin Franklin stated that nothing is certain in this world but death and taxes. The issue of paying taxes is much more significant than this statement suggests. Revenue from income, payroll, Medicare, Social Security, corporate taxes, and other receipts is the fuel that propels the federal machinery and keeps it operational.

The federal budget is a big deal because not only does it concern our money but it also directly affects us all. This budget determines how our money will be spent on everything, from defense, education, communities, health care, law enforcement, Social Security, roads, and bridges, to advancing science and technology, and much more. Money generated at the state level also goes into the kitty that pays for many of these activities. The vast majority of what is paid to the federal government is returned to communities, corporations, nonprofits, small businesses, and individuals in the form of loans, contracts, grants, and cooperative agreements. Currently, programs that support communities, nonprofits, and universities get about twelve cents of every federal dollar spent. Medicaid, Medicare, Social Security, defense/security, and payment on the national debt get the other eighty-eight cents for every dollar spent. Making money stretch and saving a little on the side is a lofty goal for most individuals. Likewise, efforts to make ends meet at the national level are reflected in the rising national debt, which exceeded 16 trillion dollars in the fall of 2013.

Power Point ⇨ Worlds of Debt

What does a trillion dollars look like? Visualize one-dollar bills stretched end to end around the equator 2.72 times (then multiply that by 16 to get a picture of where we are). Source: CNBC.com

Federal Budget Basics

Federal spending falls into two categories: discretionary and mandatory. In 2013, the annual budget for the United States approached 3.8 trillion dollars.

Is it true mandatory programs account for most federal expenditures?

Yes, that's true. A majority of federal resources are designated for entitlement programs that support low-income, elderly, and disabled Americans. The major programs, such as Social Security, Medicare and Medicaid, and veterans' benefits, annually account for 55 to 60 percent of total federal spending. Paying for these programs is mandated by long-standing statutes, leaving less than 45 percent, or roughly 1.35 trillion dollars, for Congress to use how it sees fit.

Are defense and security considered mandatory?

Not at all. Federal funding for the military and homeland security is considered discretionary, as it is for several other nondefense programs.

Within the discretionary accounts, is it true that we spend more on defense and security than on anything else?

Yes, that's very true. Discretionary falls into two major groups: defense (29.2 percent of the total 2011 budget) and everything else we care about (14.4 percent of federal funding spent in 2011). Considering only discretionary spending, the amount for defense is almost double the amount spent on all other domestic activities combined. Outside of defense, the domestic discretionary programs, in order of budget size, are education, highways and other ground transportation, agriculture, housing assistance, biomedical research, federal law enforcement, public health services, and air traffic and related transportation.

Which communities are most likely to get discretionary money?

Domestic discretionary federal spending provides significant assistance to state and local governments and corporations and nonprofits, and it helps fill the gaps when state and local tax revenues and other funding are not sufficient.

From 2001 to 2008, growth in payments for defense and security outpaced those for all other programs, including the entitlement programs. The Center on Budget and Policy Priorities (CBPP) found that the defense/security category grew *four times* as rapidly as did all domestic programs—Social Security, Medicare, Medicaid, other entitlements and domestic discretionary programs—combined. Even more notable, funding trends over the eight years of the most recent Bush administration reflected a decline in federal funding for domestic discretionary programs except defense and security. Federal expenditures related to defense and security actually increased significantly throughout the Bush administration.

The President's Budget

Typically on the first Monday of February, the federal budget process begins when the president submits to Congress his/her vision for spending in the country's next fiscal year for approval.

Which office in the White House is responsible for the president's budget?

The Office of Management and Budget (OMB), working collaboratively with every federal department and agency, takes the lead in preparing the president's budget.

The OMB is the largest office within the Executive Office of the President. The budget request covers all federal executive departments and independent agencies.

When does Congress begin to act on the president's budget?

Congressional consideration begins once the president submits a budget request. The president's request is given in an extensive proposal of the administration's policy and spending priorities for the following year. The budget proposal includes volumes of supporting information intended to persuade Congress of the necessity and value of giving the president what he wants.

To what extent do federal agencies participate in the budget process?

Each federal executive department and independent agency will also provide additional detail to Congress on its own funding requests. These materials are known as "agency budget justifications." Every agency budget and the president's budget can be found online. Go to the specific agency's website for agency justifications, or visit www.gpo.gov or www.whitehouse.gov/omb/budget/2014.

Why should I care about this process?

The budgeting process provides a real opportunity to hold elected officials and politicians accountable for campaign promises and other community commitments.

When is the best time to let the White House know what I want to see included in the president's budget?

Most people choose to engage at the national level following the president's budget submission to Congress. But let me tell you a secret: you do not have to wait for the budget to be completed to engage. In fact, good times to engage are when folks are running for office and while the White House is drafting its proposal. Anytime from May to November of any year is a good time to communicate with the agencies, the White House, and the OMB about the budget for the following year.

Isn't Congress required to adopt a budget too?

After the president submits his proposal, Congress must draft a budget resolution. This establishes spending limits and funding caps, setting the parameters of what can be awarded through the appropriations process. The budget committees in the House and Senate are responsible for drafting budget resolutions. Congressional budget measures may accept, reject, or modify priorities outlined by the president. Budget resolutions are intended to be approved by mid-April, but adoption may occur later in the congressional calendar.

What happens after the president's budget is submitted and congressional budget resolutions are approved?

Once federal spending limits are finalized by a binding budget resolution, the House and Senate Appropriations Committees and their relevant subcommittees then approve individual appropriations bills to allocate funding to various federal programs for the following fiscal year, which begins October 1. If the individual bills are not passed and signed by the president prior to October 1, a continuing resolution or omnibus appropriations bill will be used as potential funding vehicles. Recall again, in the fall of 2013, the world witnessed the dastardly effects associated with failing to have a budget and spending bill in place. The shutdown cost the US $24 billion, not to mention the emotional toll it took on families, business owners, and workers whose incomes are tied to federal funding.

Debts and Deficits

Basic math: America's budget woes are a sign of some deep challenges that will take years to fix. We're simply spending more than we are making as a nation. Whether you embrace austerity (cutting programs) or Keynesian approaches (increasing spending as a shot in the arm), any long-term solution must be tied to job creation and a more robust engagement of highly skilled American workers and small businesses that drive innovation and productivity. These times remind me of watching a tsunami roll in. This thing we are in, this global circumstance of decline, must run its course. Many economic forecasts paint a bleak picture through 2025. It took longer than two years to dig the hole we are in, and it will take more than a few years to get out of it. No easy outs. Looking ahead, correcting this disequilibrium, just like the aftermath of a tsunami, will take time, coordinated strategies, and hard work.

America's budget challenges do not exist in a vacuum. They have many contributing factors and forces: banking crises, health care concerns, education reform, global competition, changing demographics, a downward-turning economy, veterans returning from war, persistent and pronounced unemployment, and politics gone wild. Nobel Prize winner and author Joseph Stiglitz observes in *Freefall*: "The failures in our financial system are emblematic of broader failures in our economic system, and the failures of our economic system reflect deeper problems in our society." It seems any effort to realign America's budget and economy must be done in a way that addresses deeper societal issues, particularly as these issues relate to job creation. American corporations, entrepreneurs, and workers must retool, and entrepreneurs and workers from diverse backgrounds must be constructively engaged, potentially with a combination of tax incentives and targeted spending.

Even more compelling is the issue of balancing the national budget without destabilizing industries, families, and communities. Which favored program gets cut first? Yours? Mine? Let's cut to the chase—it really is a question of which communities and groups of interests will be targeted to suffer the greatest inconvenience. Remember, outside of spending for mandatory programs and defense and security, the remaining domestic discretionary programs receive *only* about twelve to fourteen cents of every tax dollar that comes to Washington. If every program in this category were eliminated, two-thirds of the savings would have to be applied toward the interest on our national debt, leaving very little to pay the debt itself.

What is the difference between our national debt and our annual deficits?

The national debt is the total amount of money the government owes to folks who underwrite the debt, including members of the public and, to a lesser extent, foreign countries. Both groups are allowed to buy government-backed notes known as treasury bills. Similarly, the federal budget deficit is the yearly amount of spending that exceeds revenue. Add up all the deficits (and subtract those few budget surpluses we've had) for the past two-hundred-plus years, and you'll get the current national debt, not including interest. Until we begin to reduce the debt, we are kicking the proverbial can down the road.

What is a debt limit?

In 1917, the Second Liberty Bond Act allowed Congress to set limits to restrict the total federal debt, which it has done eight times since 2001. Federal debt includes public debt and debts held by government accounts, which include federal trust funds, like Social Security and Medicare. Debt limits allow the US Treasury to manage the country's finances and allow Congress to control the federal purse.

The nation began its descent into a black hole in 2002, shortly after President George W. Bush took office. When President Bill Clinton left office, the nation had a surplus exceeding 200 billion dollars. With the one-two punch of going to war and cutting taxes at about the same time, it took just a few years to tether a 12-trillion-dollar ball and chain of national debt to our economy. By 2008, the economy was in a recession and potential free fall after a series of crises. Like salve on a boil, President Obama implemented several relief, recovery, and reinvestment measures that required additional spending to bail us out and stimulate the economy. By August of 2011, Congress needed to increase the debt limit, which had maxed out at 14.3 trillion dollars. The Budget Control Act (the Debt Deal) was enacted, increasing the debt cap by 2.1 trillion dollars through spending cuts in the amount of the increase in the caps.

What happens if the United States defaults on its debt by failing to raise the debt limit or otherwise?

Experts debate the full ramifications of failure to raise the debt ceiling. However, it's safe to say if America can't pay the people and the countries it owes, it risks being regarded globally as a deadbeat. In August 2011, Standard & Poor downgraded the US credit rating. This shift had no real measurable impact. In fact, within days after the downgrade, demand for US Treasury bills increased. Others predicted a stock market collapse. That did not happen either. It's difficult to say exactly what would happen, as similar predictions accompanied the debate over going off the gold standard, for example, and America's financial standing remained strong then.

Who shoulders the burden of paying the debt?

We do. Federal income taxes must be raised to pay off the debt. Now, the "we" in "we do" means different things to different people. Some argue the rich should pay a greater share of their incomes to offset federal debt. Others, like Tea Partiers, argue the federal government must cut programs and run a smaller version of the government to dig America out of its current debt hole.

How long has there been a problem with the nation's budget?

Many presidents have struggled with managing escalating national debt, going back to Franklin Roosevelt and covering every administration since. The issue has received significant attention during the twenty-plus years I have worked at the federal level, dating back to the presidency of Ronald Reagan. For many years, I wrote numerous articles on the issue. In 2001, as a contributing columnist to *Turning Point Magazine*, I wrote in "Feast and Famine: Implications of the Bush Tax Proposal":

> Brace yourself for the pain. The tax cut train is about to leave the station. And guess what? The majority of African-American and Hispanic families with children will end up with zilch, as in zero . . . nada . . . absolutely nothing. In fact, for years to come, many Americans (red, black, white and brown) may end up with paltry crumbs, while a select few feast on the fat of the land.

In 2002, in another *Turning Point Magazine* article, "Escalating Deficits and Other Games of Chance," I wrote:

> The conclusive findings . . . are pretty consistent:
>
> (1) a fiscal crisis is developing in the United States; (2) the crisis has resulted in large part because of declining revenue related to Bush tax cuts, an anemic economy and new expenditures related to defense and homeland security; (3) deficits matter; (4) the risks of inaction are unsustainably and unbearably high; and (5) the time to act is now.

Now, more folks are recognizing the implications of current tax and spending practices.

What next?

As I stated in the 2002 article quoted previously:

> It is clear many federal policymakers are inclined to articulate and pursue a plan to bring greater balance to the budget. Stay alert. Holy Grail programs for conservatives (defense) and liberals (Social Security, Medicare, Medicaid, etc.) may be offered for the chopping block, along with other programs of relevance to states and community interests across the nation. Every American should be prepared to monitor this process. The discussions unfolding . . . will determine what programs and community interests receive funding for years to come. In this instance, having a seat at the table may help to ensure your favorite program is not served as lunch.

APPENDIX E

Making Laws and Making Them Mean Something

Who makes laws?

The US Congress has the lead responsibility to pass legislation known as "bills." Every year Congress debates thousands of bills, but on average only a few hundred are ever enacted into law. Bills are proposed by state legislators, special interest groups, and even private citizens. Under the First Amendment of the US Constitution, the people have a right to peaceful assembly and to petition the government for redress of grievances.

Where can I find the status of a bill?

Visit thomas.gov. You can search legislation by keywords, sponsoring members' names, and bill numbers.

Who writes the law?

A bill may come from many sources, and by the time it is considered on the House or Senate floor, it usually has been shaped by the input of various persons. Most commonly, a senator or representative may draft original legislation, but in other instances, a trade association or private citizen may request that a bill be prepared and help write it. Members of Congress also get help from staffers and lawyers to get the language and intent right. Once written, "the author" of the bill will seek cosponsors among colleagues to add greater credibility to the initiative, a strength-in-numbers approach.

How does a bill get introduced?

Only a senator or representative can introduce a bill for consideration. Once introduced in the Senate or House, a bill is then assigned a number, and its title and sponsors are published in the *Congressional Record*. A House bill is designated by "H.R." and the number; Senate bills are designated with an "S" prefix. This marks the beginning of a sometimes long and winding road for a bill, many of which fall by the wayside in this process.

What happens to a bill after it is introduced?

Each bill goes through intense scrutiny. It first is referred to the committee or subcommittee in charge of the topic covered by the bill, or it is referred to two or more committees that may share jurisdiction. For example, an energy conservation bill may go through the Senate Committee on Energy and Natural Resources or one of its subcommittees, such as the Senate Subcommittee on Water and Power.

At this point, the committee chairperson decides whether a bill sees the light of day by allowing it to get "reported out" of committee, meaning elected officials study and discuss it to judge the merit of the big idea the bill represents. Or, a bill can languish, going nowhere until it's clear it will never become a law.

Does a bill always go to subcommittee, and are hearings always required?

No. A bill does not always get referred to a subcommittee, and hearings are not always required. However, in many instances, subcommittee consideration is preferred because the members of these subcommittees typically have expertise in the topics the bill covers and can make better decisions as a result. Also, a subcommittee might hold hearings on the bill and invite testimony from public witnesses. Many witnesses are executive branch officials, experts, or potentially affected parties from trade associations, labor unions, academia, public interest groups, the business community, or just regular folks from back home who have an interest in or relationship to the issue.

Those not invited to testify can make their views known by writing a letter to the committee, providing a written statement, or working with national groups and consultants to make sure their viewpoints are heard.

Why is marking up a bill important?

Once hearings are completed, the subcommittee may meet to "mark up" the bill, the process of proposing and considering amendments to the bill as written. These amendments allow political parties to either improve a bill or to strategically weaken or strengthen it. The subcommittee then votes on whether to report the bill favorably to the full committee, another way of saying, "This is a good idea. Please take a look."

If it's not favorably reported, the bill dies.

What happens at the full committee?

The full committee may repeat any or all of the subcommittee's actions: hearing, markup, and vote. If the committee votes favorably, the bill will move to the full House of Representatives or the full Senate, depending on which chamber is considering the bill. If the bill never gets reported out, it could be offered as an amendment to another measure moving to the floor for a vote, another way of saying, "This idea is just too good to pass up. Let's slip it in over here so it has a chance." Otherwise, the bill dies.

Are there exceptions to the committee process?

A bill can bypass the subcommittee stage and go straight to full committee, and there are times when a bill may be reported out of full committee and go to the floor for a vote without a hearing and markup. Procedural rules in the House and Senate govern when shortcuts can be used. The chairperson of the full committee has senior authority in managing the movement of any measure from committee to a floor vote.

Are all bills debated?

Almost every major bill will be debated. When the bill reaches the floor of the House or Senate, everybody may debate it. At this point, the bill may be further amended, referred back to committee, or voted on. There are exceptions: in the House of Representatives, a bill may be placed on a suspension calendar, and in the Senate, a bill may move absent debate when there is "unanimous consent."

What does it take to pass a bill?

In both the House and Senate, a bill must win a majority of the vote to move to the next phase. If a bill is passed by either the House or Senate, it is referred to the other chamber. A House-passed bill may be placed directly on the Senate calendar, allowing it to bypass the subcommittee and committee reviews there. Usually, however, the subcommittees and committees in both chambers have an opportunity to hold hearings and amend the bill. Related or identical legislation often proceeds through the House and Senate simultaneously.

Does it always take 50 percent plus one vote in each chamber for legislation to pass?

No. Sometimes a larger majority is required. For instance, in the Senate, sixty votes are required to break a filibuster or bypass the traditional committee process with "unanimous consent." Sixty votes also are required to override a presidential veto.

What if the House and Senate bills are identical?

If a bill is passed in identical form by the House and Senate, it is delivered to the president.

How are any differences in House and Senate bills resolved?

If there are differences between the House and Senate versions of the bill, a conference committee is appointed by leadership of both chambers to resolve the differences. If the conferees are unable to reach agreement, the legislation dies. If they do reach an agreement, the bill is sent back to both chambers, which must vote on the compromise without further amendment.

What happens when the bill is sent to the president for review?

If the House and Senate approve the conference committee bill, it goes to the president for further action. The president has four options: sign the bill into law; take no action while Congress is in session, in which case the bill becomes law after ten days; take no action while the Congress is in final adjournment, in which case the bill dies (known as a "pocket veto"); or veto the bill.

What happens if the president vetoes a bill?

If the president vetoes a bill, Congress may attempt to override the veto. This requires a two-thirds majority vote by both the House and Senate. If either fails to achieve a two-thirds majority in favor of the legislation, the bill dies. If both succeed, the bill becomes law.

How are laws implemented?

Enactment of any law requires federal agency review and executive branch enforcement. Once a new law has been enacted, the relevant federal agency is authorized by Congress to create the regulations needed to make the law work. Seldom will Congress provide the details on how major bills should be enforced, so federal agencies establish regulations that define exactly what's legal and what's not under the law. For example, regulations created by the EPA to implement the Clean Air and Clean Water Acts identify what types and levels of pollutants are safe and which constitute violations of federal law. The agency sets guidelines and penalties associated with compliance and enforcement. The agency can also launch public awareness campaigns to educate citizens and affected industries.

APPENDIX F
What's an Authorization Bill?

*Even when laws have been written down, they ought not
always to remain unaltered.* — *Aristotle*

When people mention a bill, it's likely to be what is known as an *authorization bill,* which creates, establishes, modifies, or defines a new or existing program or policy directive. Ideally, laws passed in Congress should solve problems or create a better way of life for Americans. There are times, however, when laws benefit only narrowly defined groups or interests, or even hurt certain communities.

Power Point ⇨ Examples

The Civil Rights Act, the Voting Rights Act, the Equal Pay Act, the Clean Air and Clean Water Acts, and No Child Left Behind are authorization laws that prohibit certain discriminatory practices and affect the air we breathe, the water we drink, and the quality of our schools. The Accountable Care Act (the health reform law) and any legislation to repeal it are authorization measures.

Why do I need to know what an authorization bill is?

Sometimes the solution to a problem requires creating, significantly changing, or renewing a government agency or program. Laws are required to *authorize* the proper department to establish a new program or to amend an existing one.

How long do authorization bills last?

An authorization may last for one or many years. There are short-term, long-term, and permanent authorizations. Social Security and Medicare are permanent authorizations, also known as entitlement programs.

Do authorization bills contain dollar amounts or funding levels?

It is typical for an authorization bill to limit how much can be spent on its provisions. Sometimes, exact dollar limits are included; however, more general limits are allowed by the phrase "such sums as necessary," which gives the appropriators broad discretion. More often than not, specific funding caps reflect the most desired goals: the amount of money ultimately secured through the appropriations process often is much less than the amount authorized by the law. A great deal of advocacy and input from real people like you are necessary to budget the right amount of money to make a particular law effective. Even after an authorization is passed, no money can actually be spent or committed by the program or agency unless a corresponding appropriations bill is passed into law. For instance, while funding for defense, education, housing, job training, law enforcement, and transportation programs can be authorized, no real money is available until actual dollars are appropriated, much like a check that notifies your bank to pay the grocer or gas company. It has been said that Congress can authorize NASA to send a woman to the moon but that it will take actual money to buy the gas to get her there.

Are there different types of authorization bills?

Other types of authorizations involve adopting various tax policies. It is through taxes that the majority of domestic revenue is generated to support federally approved programs. Under the Constitution, Congress takes the lead in developing any legislation related to taxing and spending. It can be said that with one hand Congress takes (taxation), and with the other, it gives away (appropriations). Tax revenues are collected in the form of individual taxes, corporate taxes, fees, and other charges paid into the US Treasury.

Where do our tax dollars go?

A majority share of what is collected is returned to states, local governments, those who contract with and provide services to the federal government (e.g., defense contractors, physicians participating in the Medicaid and Medicare programs, universities), and individual citizens and organizations in the form of grants, contracts, cooperative agreements, and entitlement spending. Most of the money you send to Washington does not stay in Washington. It is returned to industries, communities, and individual stakeholders—particularly those with vested interests in a federal policy—including regular folks belonging to every class (the rich, middle class, and poor).

APPENDIX G

What's an Appropriations Bill?

Money is not required to buy one necessity of the soul. — Henry David Thoreau

But, it sure helps to pay the bills! — My Mamma

What is an appropriations bill?

An appropriations bill is a law that allows the US Department of Treasury to release a specific amount of real dollars to pay for specific agencies, programs, and projects. The funded activity must be authorized, as no appropriations can be made for an unauthorized program or agency.

How often must an appropriations bill be considered?

Every year, although multiyear appropriations are occasionally passed. Annual appropriations require that funds appropriated to a program or agency be spent by the end of the current fiscal year.

What happens if no appropriations bill is passed?

Until an appropriations bill is passed, there is no guarantee a program will continue beyond its current year of operation. Basically, without annual appropriations, no federal agency (and the programs it manages) can operate.

The authority to write appropriations bills falls under the jurisdiction of what body?

Under Article I, Section 9 of the US Constitution, all spending bills must originate with Congress. This legislation must be signed by the president to become law.

How is appropriated funding distributed?

Once the president signs the appropriations legislation, every federal agency receives the funding it designates for general and specific activities. Most funding leaves DC and is awarded through various mechanisms, including entitlement beneficiary accounts, grants, contracts, cooperative agreements, loan guarantees, and interest payments.

What's the difference between an appropriations and authorization bill?

The appropriations bill provides for the final money to spend on certain activities. Authorization bills typically recommend how to spend the money, but they have no teeth absent a final appropriation.

There are two other major distinctions between an authorization and an appropriations bill: (1) unlike an authorization bill, which may take several years to pass, appropriations bills are acted on every year; and (2) the provisions contained in each appropriations bill have a shelf life of the period to which the appropriations apply (typically one year).

When does the appropriations process start?

Appropriations deliberations begin after the president submits his annual budget (usually in February of every year, following the State of the Union Address). Annual appropriations require that money given to the program or agency be spent by the end of the current fiscal year.

How does the appropriations process work?

Many authorized programs or agencies are created and destroyed by the amount of money they receive or don't receive through the appropriations process. An appropriations bill is drafted by a specialized subcommittee of the full Appropriations Committee. There are twelve appropriations subcommittees, with jurisdiction over every federal agency and program. Each subcommittee receives a specific allocation of money to spend. This is known as the 602(B) Allocation.

Who determines what amounts each subcommittee will receive?

Allocations under 602(B) are determined by the "cardinals," or the chairs of each of the subcommittees.

When are appropriations bills actually drafted?

Appropriations bills are written after a series of hearings that occur February through May. All the major agencies, public witnesses, and members of Congress participate in these proceedings in person or by submitting written testimony.

Are there other times in the appropriations process to influence congressional spending decisions?

The full appropriations cycle typically runs from February to September of every year. The later you wait, the harder it is to influence outcomes—it's never impossible but it is increasingly difficult. Throughout the cycle, committee members get thousands if not millions of letters from constituents supporting or opposing the full spectrum of programs under their jurisdiction. It is through this process that funding priorities ultimately are established and finalized.

When does the federal government's fiscal year begin?

The federal fiscal year begins on October 1 and ends on September 30 of the following year. Once the fiscal year ends, no more money can be spent from the appropriations made the prior year. New appropriations for the new fiscal year must be passed for continued spending.

What is a continuing resolution?

If Congress fails to enact spending legislation before October 1, an alternative is to pass a special appropriations bill known as a continuing resolution, or CR, which generally permits continued spending for a short period, usually at prior-year levels.

What other action can Congress take to keep the federal government funded when it has not passed all of the appropriations bills by the end of the fiscal year?

Congress can choose not to pass the twelve appropriations bills as separate legislative measures by folding some or all of the measures into a larger package known as an *omnibus appropriations bill.*

Why should I care?

The nature and scope of every federal program ultimately is shaped by the amount of funding provided through the appropriations process. The relevance of the budget and appropriations processes cannot be overstated.

What happens after appropriations bills become law?

The executive branch and the federal agencies falling under it take lead responsibility for distributing funds through grants, contracts, cooperative agreements, guaranteed loans, and subsidies. The awards fall under the broad categories of mandatory and discretionary accounts. Grants usually fall under the discretionary line and are classified as either competitive or formula. There are certain grants that can be awarded pursuant to an unsolicited proposal.

Power Point ⇨ The Power of the Purse

In the absence of earmarks and in the face of gridlock and inertia, the executive branch increases its relevance and role in managing how taxpayer money (federal funding) is distributed, enhancing the power and influence of the White House and executive agencies while diminishing the role of Congress in the funding chain.

APPENDIX H

What Do Lobbyists Really Do?

*Okay, you've convinced me. Now go out there and bring
pressure on me. — Franklin D. Roosevelt*

What is the difference between "lobbying" and "advocacy"? These terms are sometimes confused. According to the Center for Lobbying in the Public Interest:

> The definition of lobbying generally involves attempts to influence specific legislation through direct or grassroots communications with legislators or their staff. Advocacy includes lobbying but covers a much broader range of activities such as executive branch activities, issue organizing, and nonpartisan voter engagement. One way of differentiating between the two terms is to understand that lobbying always involves advocacy but advocacy does not necessarily involve lobbying.

Lobbying is narrowly focused on influencing or persuading policymakers to support a certain position related to particular legislation. Other aspects of advocacy include several components: coalition building and management, community and grassroots organizing, fundraising and development, media outreach, decision-maker advocacy, research and education, and nonpartisan voter engagement. When properly engaged and informed, these activities can be used by folks like you and me to tackle some of the most daunting challenges affecting individuals, communities, corporations, and nonprofits. During the past few years, the field of lobbying has generated a great deal of attention. Members of the profession have been called hired guns, hookers, whores, prostitutes, and pimps. Lobbyists often are seen as evildoers who have ransomed deeply rooted American values related to the common good and equity for the cost of corporate efficiency and greed. Lobbyists, more than any other group, are held responsible for controlling the purse strings of policymakers and "fleecing" working folks. Some would have you believe that lobbyists feast on milked Indian tribes and snack on the stem-cell blood of babies. These assertions deliberately are over the top. Like most professions, the industry does have a set of unique challenges. But if you really think about it, lobbyists work for particular industries or interests and serve as an extension of those they represent.

While many have heard about lobbyists, few truly understand what they do and even fewer have ever met one. There are two types of lobbyists: (1) good lobbyists (*white hats*) and (2) bad lobbyists (*black hats*). Recall the image of the lobbyist who flew too close to the sun, the infamous Jack Abramoff. Remember the black fedora and trench coat he modeled during his trial on federal fraud, corruption, and related charges. The line between the types is neither exact nor absolute, and which type a lobbyist is often depends on which side you're on. Mostly, the issues a lobbyist represents, rather than the industry pushing the effort, determine the classification. President Obama himself seems to have struggled with drawing a clear line. He had this to say about lobbyists and "special interests" in his book *The Audacity of Hope*:

> I've never been entirely comfortable with the term "special interests," which lumps together ExxonMobil and bricklayers, the pharmaceutical lobby and the parents of special-ed kids. Most political scientists would probably disagree with me, but to my mind, there's a difference between a corporate lobby whose clout is based on money alone, and a group of like-minded individuals—whether they be textile workers, gun aficionados, veterans or family farmers—coming together to promote their interests; between those who use their economic power to magnify their political influence far beyond what their numbers might justify, and those who are simply seeking to pool their votes to sway their representatives. The former subvert the very idea of democracy. The latter are its essence.

Where do lobbyists work?

Lobbyists fall into several classifications. The major ones are law firms with lobbying shops, corporate lobbyists, and independent (or contract) lobbyists. Law firms work for clients in the for-profit and nonprofit sectors, including major corporations, small businesses, municipalities, state governments, and trade and industry associations. Corporate lobbyists are employed by and represent corporations, such as GM, Google, Viacom, Nike, and Coca-Cola. Independent, or contract, lobbyists, the type often depicted and mentioned in popular media, strictly lobby. Unlike law firms, independent lobbying firms do not practice law and typically are not involved with regulatory matters. For a retainer fee, these lobbyists lobby on single or multiple public policy issues. They work in firms that range in size and revenue from the multimillion-dollar entities that populate K Street to one-person shops.

How old is the practice of lobbying?

Lobbying can be traced to the earliest days of Congress. Numerous written accounts of lobbying activity were recorded in the 1790s.

What is the relationship between lobbying and the US Constitution?

Under the First Amendment of the US Constitution, citizens have a right to speak up. It states, "Congress shall make no law abridging the freedom of speech, or of the press; or the right of the people peaceably to assemble, and to petition the Government for a redress of grievances." Lobbying, then, is associated with the right of free speech and the right every American has to petition the government and to assemble peacefully.

Who coined the term "lobbyist"?

Washington lore asserts that the word came into being during the administration of Ulysses S. Grant. When people wanted to bend the ear of President Grant, they might have sought him at the historic Willard Hotel on Pennsylvania Avenue across from the White House. People seeking jobs, contracts, and particular positions in legislation would approach him in the lobby. Grant is said to have referred to them as "those damned lobbyists." The late Robert C. Byrd in an exposé appearing on the US Senate website notes that lobbying dates back to the earliest days of the US Congress and the 1790s. Even before that, the word *lobbies* has been associated with the English House of Commons as far back as the 1640s.

How is lobbying relevant?

The lobbying profession derives relevance in three ways:

Politics: The United States is founded on democratic principles that favor a broad representation of voices.

Mathematics: The 535 members of Congress represent more than 300 million people.

Economics: Lobbying efforts increase the competitiveness of an idea in the marketplace of ideas.

How many lobbyists work in Washington, DC?

Lobbying has changed significantly in the past few decades. In *Supercapitalism*, former US Labor Secretary Robert B. Reich notes that during the 1950s, fewer than one hundred companies maintained a presence in Washington. By the 1990s, the number had grown to five hundred. Estimates of the exact number of people currently engaged in lobbying at the federal level vary, but the number quoted most often is about thirty-two thousand. That is a little less than one lobbyist for about every ten thousand people.

How much money is spent on lobbying?

According to the Center for Responsive Politics, the total amount spent on lobbying in 2007 reached about 2.7 billion dollars. This is substantially more than the 1.45 billion dollars spent in 1998, without adjusting for inflation.

How much do lobbyists make?

Annual salaries range from around $70,000 to many millions. Thousands of lobbyists make less than $100,000 annually. Those who command $250,000 or more a year are able to do so because of two factors: what they know in reference to the policy issue they are engaged in to shape or influence and who they know in Congress, including both members and their staffs, and the executive branch. The more breadth and depth a lobbyist possesses in these areas, the higher that person's pay.

Can I lobby if I have relationships but no experience or vice versa?

The best lobbyists have both sets of attributes. Having one without the other can get a person to a certain point, but running with the big dogs requires a combination of both. That is to say, having some game, hustle, and strong political relationships will kick open some doors, but the absence of an understanding of the issue, the federal process, or both will undermine your other strengths. Similarly, an individual may be the most knowledgeable person in the world on an issue, but absent any relationship with policymakers—elected officials, agency personnel, or congressional staff—translating that knowledge into a federal policy, program, or action is highly improbable.

Are there any federal laws that apply to lobbying?

By law, lobbyists in Washington, DC, are required to register their names, client information, and items that are the targets of their efforts with Congress. The Lobbying Disclosure Act (LDA), as amended, now requires lobbyists to register "no later than 45 days after a lobbyist first makes a lobbying contact or is employed or retained to make a lobbying contact, whichever is earlier, such lobbyist shall register with the Secretary of the Senate and the Clerk of the House of Representatives."

How does the LDA define "lobbyist"?

The law provides a specific and official definition of who and what a lobbyist is. The act says: "The term lobbyist means any individual who is employed or retained by a client for financial or other compensation for services that include more than one lobbying contact, other than an individual whose lobbying activities constitute less than 20 percent of the time engaged in the services provided by such individual to that client over a six-month period."

Does this definition of lobbying apply to all persons meeting the criteria?

Certain people and entities are exempt from filing and reporting, including media professionals, public officials (elected, appointed, or employees of a federal, state, or local unit of government in the United States), and those who are retained for less than $12,000 annually. More detailed analyses are compiled regularly by the Center on Responsive Politics and published primarily through its website, opensecrets.org.

APPENDIX I
Other Key Internet Resources

Budget and Appropriations

Executive Branch:

Office of the President, White House: The Office of Management and Budget has broad oversight in developing and monitoring the president's budget priorities and related agency activity, including the administration of programs authorized and appropriated by Congress. Relevant information is at whitehouse.gov/omb, budget.gov, and gpoacess.gov/usbudget.

The President's Commission on Fiscal Responsibility: Also known as the Debt Commission or the Bowles-Simpson Commission, President Obama convened this bipartisan group in 2010 to identify a common set of solutions to America's debt and growing deficit. The commission failed to formally endorse a plan of action for fiscal sustainability, though issues identified by the group are being continually debated www.fiscalcommission.gov.

Legislative Branch:

Congressional Budget Office: A nonpartisan office reporting directly to the US Congress on matters relevant to the nation's budget; http://www.cbo.gov/.

US House of Representatives Budget Committee: The committee in the House having lead responsibility for approving broadly stated budget priorities for that particular body; budget.house.gov.

US Senate Budget Committee: The committee in the Senate with lead responsibility for approving broadly stated budget priorities for that particular body; budget.senate.gov.

US House of Representatives Appropriations Committee: The committee in the House responsible for appropriating designated funding for every federal agency and program on an annual basis; appropriations.house.gov.

US Senate Appropriations Committee: The committee in the Senate that shares jurisdiction with the House committee over providing actual funding for every federal agency and program; appropriations.senate.gov.

Nonprofits:

Center on Budget Policy and Priorities: cbpp.org; Center for American Progress: americanprogress.org

Joint Center for Political & Economic Studies: jointcenter.org

Earmarks:

During those legislative cycles when earmarks are permitted, each member of Congress is required to post a listing of earmark requests on his or her website, which is linked on senate.gov or house.gov.

Grant Information and Funding Opportunities:

Catalog of Federal Domestic Assistance Programs (CFDA): CFDA provides a full listing of federal programs available to state and local governments (including the District of Columbia); federally recognized Indian tribal governments; territories and possessions; domestic public, quasipublic, and private profit and nonprofit organizations and institutions; specialized groups; and individuals; cfda.gov.

Federal grants: grants.gov, the place to find and apply for federal grant money electronically. This site does not provide access to information that may be classified as personal financial assistance.

The Federal Register, www.federalregister.gov, provides notices of agency rule makings, competitive grant funding opportunities, public hearings, and other matters falling under the jurisdiction of the executive branch and the federal agencies.

Official US Government Portal, usa.gov, serves as a portal for all government information, services, and transactions. You can find pretty much anything on this site: student loan information, mortgage calculators, information on organ and tissue donor registries, and the list goes on.

Lobbyist information

One-stop resource: opensecrets.org

Congressional lobby reports: disclosure.senate.gov

Foreign agent registration: usdoj.gov

Leadership directories: leadershipdirectories.com (for a fee)

Washington representatives directory: lobbyistsinfo.com (for a fee)

Acknowledgments

Thanks to the Almighty Creator, the maker of all things perfect and good. I also want to acknowledge the support of those from my hometown, Decatur, Illinois. It was through them that I first learned of the possibilities associated with hard work, fairness, helping others, and the pursuit of excellence.

Scores of people and experiences shaped my personal growth and understanding of the federal process. All deserve special acknowledgment, yet no one person or group can be singled out properly. For my colleagues, employers and mentors on and off of the Hill, thank you for your friendship and support. This includes colleagues at Polsinelli PC, who demonstrated generosity of spirit during the time that I wrote this book.

Thanks to the clients and communities with whom I have worked over the years for choosing to believe and daring to act. It is a humbling experience to witness the tenacity you exhibit in leadership and public service. Much of this book is attributable to experiences I gained working with you.

Many thanks to members of the Congressional Black Caucus. Other US representatives and senators with whom I have worked deserve recognition also. Republicans and Democrats; progressives, moderates, and conservatives; those representing frontier, rural, suburban, and urban communities across the nation have been equally helpful. Without the promises and the assistance they provide to their constituents, my work would be impossible.

A most special acknowledgment goes to "Sister Prez," Dr. Johnnetta B. Cole, mentor and sister-friend. Your words and acts of courage and wisdom and your commitment to equality are evidenced in the thoughts you share in the foreword of this book.

Kathie Bailey Mathae, Kimberly Rudolph, Charles Stephenson, Lydia Watts, and Veronica Webb, thank you for your priceless review, input, and friendship. Thanks to Emily Clack, Geraldine Conrad, the late Marion McGrath, and Wendy Welch-Pineda. Deep heartfelt appreciation for Huriyyah Muhammad, who dove in head first when this project was in its infancy. Kudos to Noriko McClinton and Richard and Marcie Pottern for the graphic design. Thanks to Mary Gallagher Stout for the inspiration. A special high-five goes to Deborah Douglas and Pittershawn Palmer for their word mastery and editing prowess. To the staff members who have assisted me during the years of authoring this work: Shauna Alexander, Perrin Cooke, Sumit Dasgupta, Garrett Lamm, Sarah Pilli, Malini Sen, Maximilliano Sevillia, Christian Washington, and Gabrielle Williams—thank you.

For all my extended and adopted family members and most especially for my siblings who happily poured water on their cornflakes the few mornings we had no milk: thank you for faithfully sharing the struggle and giving life to our mother's dreams. My nieces and nephews, this book really is for you and your children. My prayer is that my generation leaves the world better than we found it and that we do right by you.

For all the BFFs, LaTanya Junior stands out. LaTanya, you are a visionary, an extraordinary brand developer and strategic planner. You have been both a compass and a light. The book is much better because of you, and so am I. If no one told you they love you today, I do. Many thanks to the folks who raised you. Yes, Ruby and the late Marvin Junior, and all the members of The Dells, that means you.

Finally, many thanks to you, the reader, for taking time to read this book.

About the Author

Anita Estell is considered a trailblazer and pioneer in the Washington, DC, government affairs community and has received awards and recognition for her work and contributions in this area. She is a noted Washington attorney, lobbyist, strategist, and equity shareholder of a national law firm. Anita has spent over two decades promoting the development of affordable and widely accessible citizen-centric advocacy approaches that expand awareness, seed opportunity, and drive measurable results.

Photo by Brianna Romano

In the public sector, she has played a senior role in advising policymakers on matters related to more than $1 trillion in federal programs. In the private sector Anita has helped to secure more than $10 billion in federal funding for communities, clients, and coalitions through the adoption of federal programs and policies benefitting more than 5 million people in the United States, Africa, Haiti, and the Caribbean.

As a teenager, Anita studied freedom and learned about collective action. Advocacy and the use of public policy to strengthen communities have captured her attention and energy since then. Throughout her career, Anita has worked to broaden access to and engagement with the federal government. *The Power of Us* is in part a translation of the most profound lessons she has learned. A beneficiary of the American promise, Anita grew up near the cornfields of Central Illinois and was raised by a divorced mother of seven, who as a child picked cotton in the Mississippi Delta.

Anita has written numerous columns, owned and produced a radio show, and maintains a blog called *The People's Place* (www.anitaestellblog.com). She received her bachelor's degree in journalism and juris doctor from the University of Missouri-Columbia, where she also has been inducted into the Order of the Coif. Anita is a member of the Missouri Bar. She is active with several nonprofit and community organizations. She founded and chairs ROSA PAC, a political action committee that supports women of color in Congress. She also serves on the board of directors for the Congressional Management Foundation. Anita lives in Washington, DC, where her dog, Savannah, reminds her regularly that canines rule.

Key Definitions

Art: The sensory and perceptual pursuit and manifestation of ideals, wisdom, and wonder that reach toward or realize an aesthetic vision that inspires the intellect, or works that stir the mind, heart, body, or soul.

Citizen centricity: Of the people, for the people, and by the people.

Citizenship: The qualities that a person is expected to have as a responsible member of a community, including rights, privileges, and responsibilities.

Democracy: (1) An egalitarian form of government in which all the citizens of a nation together determine public policy, the laws, and the actions of their state, requiring that all citizens (meeting certain qualifications) have an equal opportunity to express their opinions. (2) A government in which the supreme power is vested in the people and exercised by them directly or indirectly through a system of representation usually involving periodically held free elections.

Enlightened: (1) Spiritually or intellectually insightful, alert, vibrant, and creative. The essence of "Aha!" Truth. As Thomas Jefferson stated, "Enlighten the people generally, and tyranny and oppression of body and mind will vanish like evil spirits at the dawn of day." (2) Factually well informed, tolerant of alternative opinions, and guided by rational thought.

Essence: (1) The intrinsic or indispensable properties that serve to characterize or identify something. (2) The most important ingredient; the crucial element. The soul.

Love: Love is kind. It knows neither anger nor jealousy. It has been said that love is the oxygen for the soul. Love is the river where eternity quenches its thirst and courage washes its feet. It is that place from which life springs forth passionately, purposefully, and robustly toward itself. In politics, love for each other often is missing.

Power: "Power is always associated with that which supports the significance of life itself. It appeals to that part of human nature that we call in contrast to force, which appeals to that which we call crass. Power appeals to what uplifts, dignifies and ennobles. Force must always be justified, whereas power requires no justification. Force is associated with the partial, power with the whole." —David R. Hawkins, MD, PhD.

Science: Knowledge-based endeavors that engineer, measure, research, evaluate, establish, postulate, test, prove, or produce results related to that which exists or may exist in theory or in fact.

Sources: Merriam-Webster Dictionary, Super Brain, by Deepak Chopra, MD and Rudolph E. Tanzi, PhD, *Power vs. Force: The Hidden Determinants of Human Behavior* by David R. Hawkins, The Free Dictionary by Farlex (www. thefreedictionary.com), and life experience.

Bibliography

Avner, Marcia. *The Lobbying and Advocacy Handbook for Nonprofit Organizations: Shaping Public Policy at the State and Local Level.* St. Paul, MN: Fieldstone Alliance, 2006.

Bazel, Lauren, Michael Ettinger, and Michael Linden. "A Path to Balance: A Strategy for Realigning the Federal Budget." Center For American Progress, December 2009.

Beeman, Richard, *Plain, Honest Men: The Making of the American Constitution.* New York: Random House, 2009.

Bobo, Kimberly A., JackieKendall, and Steven Max. *Organizing for Social Change: Midwest Academy Manual for Activists.* Santa Ana, CA: Seven Locks, 3rd Edition, 2001.

Bugg-Levine, Anthony, Bruce Kogut, and Nalin Kulatilaka. "A New Approach to Funding Social Enterprises." *Harvard Business Review*, January-February 2012.

Byrd, Robert C. "Lobbyists." Senate.gov: September 28, 1987; updated 1989. http://www.senate.gov.

Campbell, Joseph. *The Portable Jung.* New York: Penguin, 1976.

Carter, Rita. *The Human Brain.* New York: DK, 2009.

Chodron, Pema. *Always Maintain a Joyful Mind and Other Lojong Teachings on Awakening Compassion and Fearlessness.* Boston: Shambhala, 2007.

Chopra, Deepak. *Creating Affluence: The A-to-Z Steps to a Richer Life.* San Rafael, CA: Amber Allen and New World, 1993.

Chopra, Deepak. *Synchrodestiny.* London: Rider, 2005.

Chopra, Deepak, with Gotham Chopra. *Spiritual Laws of Superheroes.* New York: Harper One, 2011.

Chopra, Deepak and Rudolph E. Tanzi. *Super Brain.* New York: Harmony, 2012

Coburn, Thomas. "Emmett Till Unsolved Civil Rights Crime Act." *Congressional Record,* August 1, 2008.

Covey, Stephen R., A. Roger Merrill, and Rebecca R. Merrill. *First Things First.* New York: Simon & Schuster, 1994.

De Bolla, Peter. *The Fourth of July and the Founding of America.* New York: Overlook, 2007.

De Tocqueville, Alexis. *Democracy in America.* New York: The Library of America, 2004.

"Digital Nation: 21st Century America's Progress toward Universal Broadband Internet Access." *US Department of Commerce, Nation Telecommunications and Information Administration,* February 2010.

Dilanian, Ken. "Obama Showed Independent Streak in Lobbyists Dealings." *USA Today,* July 6, 2008.

Dilanian, Ken. "Lobbyists Find More Ways to Bond with Lawmakers." *USA Today*, January 31, 2008.

Doidge, Norman. *The Brain That Changes Itself.* New York: Viking, 2007.

Ellis, Joseph J. *Founding Brothers: The Revolutionary Generation.* New York: Vintage, 2000.

Estell, Anita. "Feast and Famine: Implications of the Bush Tax Proposal." *Turning Point Magazine*, Summer 2001.

Estell, Anita. "Escalating Deficits and Other Games of Chance." *Turning Point Magazine*, November/December 2002.

Fitch, Bradford. *Citizen's Handbook to Influencing Elected Officials: Citizen Advocacy in State Legislatures and Congress.* Alexandria, VA: TheCapitol.Net, 2010.

Fox, Leslie M. and Priya Helweg. *"Advocacy Strategies for Civil Society: A Conceptual Framework and Practitioners Guide." USAID Contract AED 5468-1-00-6013-00,* August 31, 1997.

Franklin, John Hope. *From Slavery to Freedom*, 8th ed. New York: Knopf, 2009.

Friedman, Thomas L. *The World Is Flat: A Brief History of the Twenty-First Century.* New York: Farrar, Straus and Giroux, 2006.

Gawain, Shakti. *Creative Visualization.* Navato, CA: New World Library, 2008.

Gelak, Deanna R. *Lobbying and Advocacy.* Alexandria, VA: TheCapitol.Net, 2008.

Gladwell, Malcolm. *The Tipping Point: How Little Things Can Make a Big Difference.* New York: Little Brown, 2000.

Gold, Martin B. *Senate Procedure and Practice.* Oxford: Rowman & Littlefield, 2008.

Goldschmidt, Kathy and Leslie Ochreiter. "Communicating with Congress: How the Internet Has Changed Citizen Engagement." Commissioned by the Congressional Management Foundation and Zogby International, 2008.

Hamilton, Lee. *How Congress Works.* Bloomington: Indiana University Press, 2004.

Hamilton, Lee. "You Need to Know Lobbying." Center on Congress, March 13, 2008.

Hamilton, Roger. *Your Life Your Legacy: An Entrepreneur Guide to Finding Your Flow.* Singapore: Achievers International, 2010.

Hanna, Edward, Henry Hicks and Ted Koppel. *The Wit and Wisdom of Adlai Stevenson.* New York: Hawthorn, 1965.

Hawkins, Betsy Wright. *Setting Course: A Congressional Management Guide*, 6th ed. Washington, DC: Congressional Management Foundation, 1998.

Hawkins, David R. *Power vs. Force: The Hidden Determinants of Human Behavior.* Carlsbad, CA: Hay House, 2002.

Hill, Napoleon. *Think and Grow Rich.* Los Angeles: Highroads Media, 2004.

Holder, Jackie. *Soul Purpose.* London: Piatkus, 1999.

Isaacson, Walter. *Einstein: His Life and Universe.* New York: Simon & Schuster, 2007.

Jung, C. G. *Four Archetypes.* Princeton, New Jersey: First Princeton/Boligen, Paperback reissue, 2010.

Kabat-Zinn, Jon. *Full Catastrophe Living.* New York: Delta, 2009.

Kanter, Rosabeth Moss. *America the Principled.* New York: Crown, 2007.

King, Martin Luther, Jr. *The Words of Martin Luther King, Jr.,* 2nd ed. New York: Newmarkets, 1984.

Lipton, Bruce H. *The Biology of Belief: Unleashing the Power of Consciousness, Matter, and Miracles,* 7th ed. Carlsbad, CA: Hay House, 2009.

Loeb, Paul Rogat. *Soul of a Citizen.* New York: St. Martin's Griffin, 2010.

Mann, Thomas E., and Norman Ornstein. *The Broken Branch: How Congress Is Failing America and How to Get It Back on Track.* New York: Oxford, 2006.

New World Bible Translation Committee, New World Translation of the Holy Scriptures 2004.

Oakley, Ed, and Doug Krug. *Enlightened Leadership: Getting to the Heart of Change.* New York: Fireside, 1994.

Obama, Barack. *The Audacity of Hope.* New York: Crown, 2006.

Peck, M. Scott. *The Road Less Traveled: A New Psychology of Love, Traditional Values, and Spiritual Growth.* New York: Touchstone, 2003.

Petersen-Pew Commission. "Red Ink Rising: A Call to Action to Stem the Mounting Federal Debt." December 2009.

Ramo, Joshua Cooper. *The Age of the Unthinkable.* New York: Little, Brown, 2009.

Raphael, Ray. *Founding Myths.* New York: The New Press, 2004.

Reich, Robert. *Supercapitalism.* New York: Knopf, 2007.

Roberts, Cokie. *Founding Mothers.* New York: Harper Perennial, 2005.

Rochin, Refugio I. and Lionel Fernandez. "U.S. Latino Patriots: From the American Revolution to Afghanistan, An Overview." Julian Samora Research Institute, Michigan State University, 2005.

Rosenthal, Alan. *The Third House.* Washington, DC: CQ Press, 2001.

Schneider, Judy, Michael Koempel and contributing author Robert Kieth. *Congressional Deskbook.* Alexandria, VA: TheCapitol.Net, 2012.

Selig Center for Economic Growth, Terry College of Business, University of Georgia, July 2008.

Singer, Michael A. *The Untethered Soul.* Oakland, California: New Harbinger, 2007.

Staples, Lee. *Roots to Power: A Manual for Grassroots Organizing,* 2nd ed. Westport, CT: Praeger, 2004.

Stiglitz, Joseph E. *Freefall*. New York: W. W. Norton & Company, 2010.

"The Response to Rape: Detours on the Road to Equal Justice," A Majority Staff Report Prepared for the Senate Judiciary Committee, 103rd Congress, First Session, US Government Printing Office, May 1993.

Tolle, Eckhart. *The Power of Now: A Guide to Spiritual Enlightenment*. Navato, CA: Namaste and New World, 2004.

Tolle, Eckhart. *A New Earth: Awakening Your Life's Purpose*. London: Plume, 2006.

Trafzer, Clifford E. *American Indians/American Presidents*. New York: Harper Collins and the Smithsonian, 2009.

Tzu, Lao, translated by Stephen Mitchell. *Tao Te Ching*. London: Frances Lincoln, 1999.

Vance, Stephanie. *Citizens in Action: A Guide to Influencing Government*. Bethesda, MD: Columbia Books, 2009.

Williamson, Marianne. *Healing the Soul of America*. New York: Touchstone, 2000.

Zinn, Howard. *A Power Governments Cannot Suppress*. San Francisco: City Lights, 2007.

Zinn, Howard. *A People's History of the United States*. New York: Harper Perennial Modern Classics, 2005.

Zukav, Gary. *The Seat of the Soul*. New York: Fireside, 1990.

Internet Sources	
america.gov	omb.gov
blackpast.org	opm.gov
bls.gov	pedaids.org (Elizabeth Glaser Pediatric Aids Institute)
change.org	senate.gov
createjobsforusa.org	thefreedictionary.com
google.com	thecajuns.com
house.gov	thomas.gov
msn.com	usa.gov
nwhm.org (National Women's History Museum)	wikipedia.com

Index